Oliver Cromwell

Be gone you rogues
you haue Sate long enough

THE BRITISH LIBRARY
HISTORIC LIVES

Oliver Cromwell

Peter Gaunt

NEW YORK UNIVERSITY PRESS
Washington Square, New York

For Dennis and Audrey

Cover illustration:
Miniature of Cromwell by
Samuel Cooper, dated 1649.
National Portrait Gallery

Half-title page illustration:
Miniature of Cromwell, also by
Samuel Cooper, dating from
the 1650s.
Private collection

Title-page illustration:
Detail of Cromwell dismissing the
Rump, from a Dutch print, 1653.
British Museum

First published in 2004 by
The British Library
96 Euston Road
London NW1 2DB

Designed and typeset
by Andrew Barron @ thextension

Printed in Hong Kong
by South Sea International Press

First published in the U.S.A.
in 2004 by
NEW YORK UNIVERSITY PRESS
Washington Square, New York
www.nyupress.org

Text © Peter Gaunt 2004
Illustrations © The British Library
Board and other named copyright
holders 2004

Library of Congress Cataloging-in-
Publication Data
Gaunt, Peter.
Oliver Cromwell/Peter Gaunt.
p. cm. – (Historic lives)
Includes bibliographical references
and index.
ISBN 0-8147-3164-3 (alk. paper)
1. Cromwell, Oliver, 1599-1658.
2. Generals—Great Britain—
Biography. 3. Heads of state—
Great Britain—Biography. 4. Great
Britain—History—Puritan
Revolution, 1642-1660—Biography.
I. Title. II. Series.

DA426.G38 2004
941.06'4'092—dc22   2004049935
[B]

The British Library
HISTORIC LIVES SERIES:

Horatio Lord Nelson
Brian Lavery

Queen Elizabeth I
Susan Doran

T.E. Lawrence
Malcolm Brown

Winston Churchill
Stuart Ball

Sir Francis Drake
Peter Whitfield

Contents

Preface

In the early seventeenth century, England seemed strong, stable and united. When Queen Elizabeth I, the last Tudor monarch, died childless in 1603, the throne passed peacefully to her distant cousin, James Stuart, already James VI of Scotland, who became King James I of England and the first of the Stuart line. On his death in 1625, the throne passed to his son, King Charles I. This hereditary monarchy possessed enormous power to run the state, oversee government and control the Church of England, the Protestant state church which had been established in the sixteenth century with the Reformation. The monarch summoned parliaments, at his own will, to advise on some areas of policy and consent to new taxes; parliament could also propose new laws, which then needed royal assent. Parliament, then as now, was made up of two chambers, a House of Commons comprising of elected members, and a House of Lords, which comprised hereditary peers (earls, dukes, viscounts, marquises and barons) and twenty-six bishops and archbishops.

By the early seventeenth century, England had effectively absorbed Wales into a single polity and had conquered and now controlled the kingdom of Ireland. Since, from 1603, the king of England was also king of Scotland, the Stuarts now ruled three kingdoms, all of which seemed in the opening decades of the seventeenth century to be enjoying peace and stability. In 1637-42, however, this apparent harmony was shattered when all the Stuart kingdoms descended swiftly into rebellion, war and internal conflict. A major civil war in England and Wales, between armies raised by king and parliament, raged from 1642 to 1646 and erupted again in 1648. Historians disagree about the causes of these conflicts, particularly the English civil war. Areas of blame include: growing political and constitutional power struggles between crown and parliament over the running and financing of the state; growing religious struggles between those who felt the Reformation had gone far enough and those who wanted further changes to make the Church of England simpler and lower; and tensions arising when a single monarch ruled three very different kingdoms, with divergent political systems, churches, religions and cultures. However, many historians attribute much of the blame to the personal and policy failings of Charles I, who exacerbated a difficult inheritance by his devious and underhand approach to government. His clumsy attempts to expand his prerogative powers and drive through political and religious changes in all three kingdoms, and his decision after 1629 to rule without calling a parliament in England, a Personal Rule which collapsed in 1640, in the wake of rebellion in Scotland, are all seen as contributing factors.

Charles's refusal to compromise and reach a durable settlement with his English parliamentary opponents, even after he had lost the civil war in 1646, and his continuing duplicity and deviousness, which led him to make a separate deal with the Scots in 1647 and renew civil war in 1648, led the victorious parliamentary armies and their political allies to push through a revolution in the winter of 1648-49. This resulted in Charles's trial and execution, the abolition of monarchy and the House of Lords and the establishment of a republic. But thereafter the parliamentarians struggled to rebuild the state and establish a durable, stable government that would satisfy soldiers and civilians, radical reformers and those favouring a return to traditional forms. Despite solid achievements during the 1650s, especially under the Protectorate of Oliver Cromwell, these divergent aspirations and centrifugal forces produced tension and instability, which eventually overwhelmed the republican regimes and led in 1660 to the peaceful Restoration of the Stuart monarchy.

Introduction

'And if a history shall be written of these times and transactions, it will be said, it will not be denied, but that these things that I have spoken are true'
(from Cromwell's speech to his first Protectorate Parliament, January 1655)

Oliver Cromwell (1599–1658) is one of the most important figures in English and British history, a dynamic leader in the times and transactions of a formative period. A minor country gentleman in East Anglia during the 1620s and 1630s, he was lifted from obscurity by the political and military turmoil of the 1640s. He became one of the most dazzlingly successful figures within the parliamentary cause which fought the English civil war, a rapidly rising soldier and politician who, by the late 1640s, possessed the power, influence, confidence and personality to shape events. He dominated the 1650s, as perhaps the only figure who could convincingly command the parliamentary army but also underpin or lead fairly stable, constitutionally reputable civilian regimes. He rose to be head of the army and then, during the last five years of his life, head of state of a united Britain, ruling as a Lord Protector empowered and limited by written constitutions.

Cromwell's greatness and importance are easily established. He was the most consistently successful soldier, on either side, during the civil war, a man often described as a natural military genius, who played a crucial role both in crushing royalism in England and Wales and then in establishing English republican control over Ireland and Scotland. Although he had no military experience at the outbreak of war in 1642, he was carried forward by a string of victories, so that by 1645 he was second-in-command of the main parliamentary army and from 1650 overall commander-in-chief. Cromwell's political power sprang from his military position, making him by the later 1640s one of a small group of men who shaped the course and nature of the post-war settlement. He was perhaps

He was the most consistently
successful soldier, on either side,
during the civil war, a man often
described as a natural military genius.

the single most important figure in driving through the English revolution of
winter 1648–49, crucially in promoting the trial and execution of the reigning
monarch. By this time he was equally adept in the spheres of army politics and
civilian, parliamentary politics and was one of the few men possessing real
experience and influence in both. As a statesman during the 1650s he sought
to rebuild a constitution and nation shattered by civil war. As head of state
from 1653 he ran a fairly stable, ostensibly civilian regime, which restored many
traditional forms and which, with its peaceable and inclusive approach at home,
began the process of healing the divisions of the war years; abroad, his regime
was strong, interventionist and internationally respected. Yet Cromwell was also
a religious visionary, a man of God, who believed that the Lord had not only
chosen him for some special mission but had also handed him the victories
which gave him power to fulfil that divine mission. In return, Cromwell strove
during his closing years to advance a broad programme of religious and moral
reformation, displaying a burning zeal to create a better, more godly land – a zeal
which ensured that he always retained a radical edge and never became a self-
satisfied, conservative figure. Although many of his goals remained unfulfilled at
his death in 1658, and within two years were further set back by the restoration
of the Stuart monarchy, while he lived Cromwell held the divergent interests of
state, army and faith in creative tension; he was both victor of the civil war and
creator of the post-war settlement.

Just as Cromwell's enduring historical importance and stature are beyond
serious doubt, so popular and academic interest in him shows no sign of waning
centuries after his death. He is England and Britain's most closely studied head
of state, with biographies of Cromwell far outnumbering those of any monarch,
even the Virgin Queen or the legendary King Arthur. But like Arthur, he is also

a much-mythologised figure, surrounded and obscured by a body of folklore and legend. Thus in popular tradition Cromwell commanded all parliamentary troops in person and was everywhere in the civil wars, staying in more mansions than Elizabeth I at her most expansive, destroying more castles than Henry VII, gunpowder and death duties put together, desecrating parish churches on a breathtaking scale, while leaving behind him a trail of boots, gloves, armour and trinkets. But if we are to approach and evaluate the real Cromwell, to come to grips with his life and career and assess his role and significance, we must get behind the mythology and disentangle truths from half-truths and invention. We must recognise, for example, that Cromwell and troops under his direct command did on occasion attack and damage castles and churches in the 1640s, while also remembering that much of the destruction to castles and to the fabric and imagery of churches in this period came about as a result of political decisions taken by parliament, a process in which Cromwell's was just one voice and vote amongst many. Moreover, the destruction seen in the mid-seventeenth century was dwarfed by the general abandonment and decay of castles in the late medieval period and by damage to, and remodelling of, religious buildings during the sixteenth-century Protestant Reformation. Getting Cromwell right, portraying him in sharp focus, true colours and accurate context, is often difficult.

This is compounded by the surprisingly strong emotions and prejudices which Cromwell has aroused since his death and which in some quarters – especially, though not exclusively, in Ireland or amongst those of Irish descent – he still provokes. Very few people approach Cromwell in a completely neutral way, without preconceptions, and many are quick to take a pungent view. It has always been thus. In the late nineteenth century a proposal by a Liberal Prime Minister, Lord Rosebery, to erect a statue of Cromwell within the Palace of

The statue of Cromwell by Sir Hamo Thornycroft outside Westminster Hall, highly controversial when erected in the 1890s, shows a military figure, sword in one hand and bible in the other, atop a towering plinth guarded by lions.
Dr Maxine Forshaw

Westminster caused deep divisions and provoked strong political opposition. The statue was eventually erected outside, before Westminster Hall, financed largely by Rosebery himself, though anonymously, and unveiled without ceremony early one November morning in 1899. Around the same time a proposal to erect a statue in Cromwell's home town of Huntingdon was thwarted by lack of public support and opposition from the local Conservative MP, though soon after a statue was erected in nearby St Ives, funded by public subscription. In the 1930s George V reportedly vetoed proposals to name a new battleship 'Cromwell', and in the 1960s Elizabeth II reportedly vetoed plans for a set of stamps to carry Cromwell's image. In the mid-twentieth century Cromwell was compared to Mussolini, Stalin and Hitler, and in more recent years to British prime ministers Thatcher and Blair, continuing a long opposition tradition of likening Cromwell to contemporary political leaders, the better to blacken the reputation of both and condemn them to ignominy.

Even in his own lifetime, Cromwell puzzled and divided his contemporaries, and starkly differing opinions emerged before and immediately after his death. To some, he was a hero, saviour of the nation and its people, a successful soldier, politician, statesman and religious visionary, who in the 1640s thwarted and turned back Stuart tyranny and then, in the 1650s, led the country towards the Promised Land, almost a second Moses advancing godliness and guiding God's chosen people towards a new Garden of Eden. But many contemporaries saw

11

Opposite: Engravings from the title
page of a pamphlet of July 1659,
published after Cromwell's death but
before the Restoration, contrast
Charles I's ghost in heaven, ornately
crowned and brightly lit, with that of
Cromwell, wandering a cave-like hell
surrounded by the fires of damnation.
From *The Court Career*, 1659.
The British Library, E989 (26)

Cromwell as an ambitious, self-seeking hypocrite who claimed to be fighting
for the rights and liberties of the people as well as for God, but who, in reality,
ruthlessly sought personal power and was only too willing to undermine or
destroy individuals or institutions – Charles I, monarchy, the Church of England,
the House of Lords, parliament itself, liberty and the rule of law, as well as former
parliamentary friends, colleagues and principles – in his grubby pursuit of
power and glory.

Although some favourable views of Cromwell circulated after the restoration
of the Stuart monarchy in 1660, especially a sneaking regard for his expansive
foreign policy and the international reputation it had won, assessments published
in the closing decades of the seventeenth century and on through the eighteenth
were predominantly unfavourable and condemnatory. Writers with strong
royalist sympathies or from the political right occasionally showed a degree of
magnanimity – to Charles II's chief minister Edward Hyde, Earl of Clarendon,
Cromwell was 'a brave bad man' who 'could never have done half that mischief
without great parts of courage, industry and judgment' – but their accounts
were overwhelmingly dark, overshadowed by Cromwell's role as king-killer and
usurper. If anything, writers sharing the more radical and reform-minded outlook
associated with the Whig political party were even more critical, condemning
Cromwell for abandoning the true parliamentary cause in the 1650s and turning
against the pursuit of liberty, instead becoming an ambitious, scheming tyrant
who as Protector betrayed and destroyed the people's rights and liberties.

Not until the early nineteenth century did the mood change. By the
Victorian period the civil war had receded into the safety of the distant historical
past, and against a background of the relative prosperity, security and stability of
Victorian Britain historians felt able to assess the civil war more dispassionately.

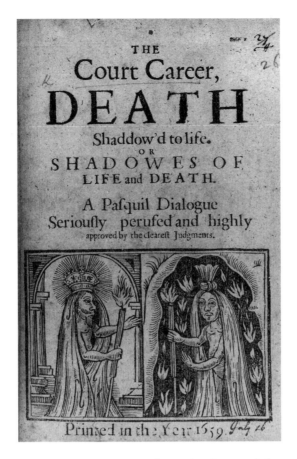

Popular and scholarly interest in Cromwell, much of it now balanced or strongly in his favour, mushroomed during the Victorian period. In the process, different groups discovered different Cromwells. For nineteenth-century trades unionists, Chartists, who likewise sought parliamentary reform, and others Cromwell was a working-class hero, a man who had stood up to a corrupt and outdated elite comprising monopolists, harsh landlords, the architects of heavy or arbitrary taxation, an unreformed parliament or an anachronistic House of Lords. For those further up the social scale he was the epitome of middle-class Victorian values, the solid farmer and self-made man who had seized opportunities for self-promotion and then offered opportunities to others through his advocacy of promotion by merit. Liberal non-conformists cast Cromwell as an opponent of a repressive state church who fought to secure religious toleration. From time to time Cromwell was claimed as forerunner and champion of other nineteenth-century causes – republicanism, socialism, imperialism – just as in the twentieth century some portrayed him as precursor of modern movements, such as fascism or Marxism. In short, we have been presented since 1800 with a wide range of images of Cromwell, some well researched and convincing, others very questionable or downright implausible. But with some exceptions, these nineteenth- and twentieth-century images have been at least evenly balanced and most have been clearly in favour of Cromwell.

Another reason for this sea change in historical opinion has been the growing reliance upon strictly contemporary source material, so viewing Cromwell in his own context. One of the earliest volumes to take this approach, *Cromwelliana*, published in 1810, brought together a range of excerpts from seventeenth-century documents – newspapers, pamphlets, letters and journals – to form a chronological account of Cromwell's life and thus provide insight into his actions and character. Far more important and ground-breaking was the appearance in 1845 of Thomas Carlyle's *Letters and Speeches of Oliver Cromwell*. Abandoning the idea of writing a biography, Carlyle instead gathered together as many of Cromwell's own writings and utterances as he could find, thus letting Cromwell speak for himself, though with plenty of commentary and interpretation thrown in. As Carlyle put it, 'it is from his own words…well read, that the world may first obtain some dim glimpse of the actual Cromwell, and see him darkly face to face'. The Cromwell his readers encountered, Carlyle thought, was 'altogether contrary to the popular fancy…not a man of falsehoods, but a man of truths'. Although Carlyle himself was critical in places and introduced pithy interjections, the tone of the volume was strongly positive and its appearance and subsequent huge popularity greatly encouraged the trend towards warmer and more favourable interpretations of Cromwell. Since that

time, all good, scholarly studies have been strongly source-based, relying
very heavily upon Cromwell's own writings and speeches and upon other
contemporary archival and documentary material relating to him. Historians
now attempt to place Cromwell in his own time and historical context rather
than force him into later, anachronistic moulds; they rely heavily upon strictly
contemporary source material and, wherever possible, they let Cromwell speak
for himself through his surviving words.

Yet there are problems with this reliance upon Cromwell's writings and
utterances. Firstly, we search in vain for any diary, autobiography, personal or
political testament or commonplace book; as far as we know Cromwell never
wrote anything like this. Secondly, although scores of Cromwell's letters survive,
giving us enormously rich insights into his actions, opinions, hopes and fears
during the war years, very few pre-date 1642 and the run of personal and
revealing letters trails off in the early 1650s. Thirdly, there survive no manuscripts
by Cromwell himself of the full texts of, or notes for, any of the major state
speeches which he delivered in the last years of his life and instead their contents
have often come down to us only via versions printed at the time by others who
probably cobbled together a text from notes made by one or more members of
the audience. Although inevitably imperfect, these texts can convey the ideas,
arguments and spirit, together with many of the actual words and phrases, of
Cromwell's orations. Fourthly, even if we focus only on the years after 1640,
when Cromwell became a figure of national importance, the surviving letters
and speeches do not provide a full and rounded picture. Even historians anxious
to view Cromwell in his own context, and as far as possible in his own words,
are compelled to cast their net more widely to encompass a range of other
seventeenth-century sources. Obvious dangers lurk. Newspaper reports could be

inaccurate, either through ignorance or by design, spreading propaganda. Some accounts of Cromwell, even those written in his own lifetime by people who were for a time colleagues or had direct dealings with him, are suspect because their authors became alienated from Cromwell and therefore had an axe to grind. Similarly, autobiographies and memoirs written, rewritten or edited for publication after Cromwell's death and the Restoration were generally coloured by hindsight, later events and the very different political and religious contexts of the later Stuart period.

One other aspect of Cromwell's letters and speeches often causes difficulties to modern readers – their language. They drip with religious and biblical allusions and references to God, in a way which our more secular age often finds rather jarring, even odd. But more than this, they are shot through with references to God's active and very physical interventions in worldly affairs and to the Lord guiding and shaping not only the unfolding events of the 1640s and 1650s but also Cromwell's own actions. Time and again, Cromwell justified his actions not on secular or what we would consider rational grounds but primarily or solely because he was obeying God's will. Cromwell claimed that he was being led by God and he ascribed many key actions – making war, giving battle, purging or ejecting of parliaments, the trial and execution of the king, his own promotion and acquisition of power, and so on – to God requiring these things and commanding Cromwell to act thus. In our far more secular age, it is all too easy to be deeply suspicious, dismiss all this as cant and hypocrisy, and argue that Cromwell was pursuing a range of entirely secular goals, military, political and perhaps also personal, and merely dressed them up in religious mumbo-jumbo, using talk of God's will as a screen to disguise or sanitise his entirely mortal will and ambition. Even some contemporaries took this view. In 1649 Richard

Overton, a member of a radical group increasingly alienated from Cromwell, claimed that 'you shall scarce speak to Cromwell about anything, but he will lay his hand on his breast, elevate his eyes, and call God to record, he will weep, howl and repent, even while he doth smite you under the first rib', while in 1655 the Venetian ambassador felt that Cromwell 'makes a great show of his zeal' and could produce tears 'at a moment's notice'. However, most modern historians are inclined to accept Cromwell's faith and his explanations of religious motivation as genuine, pointing out that the intense religious language and justifications appear in very personal letters, to members of his family and close friends, which were not intended for wider circulation, as well as in the more public letters, to the Lord General of the army or Speaker of the Commons, which he might have expected to reach a broader audience. Moreover, Cromwell accepted the logic of his stance, for if the successes and victories of the 1640s and 1650s were bestowed by God as signs of His favour upon Cromwell and the parliamentary cause, so difficulties and defeats must surely be seen as rebukes from God, evidence of disfavour. As we shall see, Cromwell did, indeed, interpret events in this way, so that setbacks stunned him and triggered uncertainty and introspection as he sought to identify the errors and sins which had offended God. Most modern historians see Cromwell's religion as fundamental during the closing decades of his life, underpinning and shaping his military and political careers.

Cromwell came to dominate the parliamentary cause which won the civil war and which then controlled the English and British state for a decade or more. Accordingly, his role, actions and approach helped to shape both the cause and the nation and he strongly influenced or determined the nature of the military victory, the ensuing revolutionary settlement and the post-war reconstruction. He is a very large and important character, about whom a great

4165 I thanke you for yor loving
lre, the same hopes & desires upon yor plant:
into my ffamily were much the same wth
me, that you expresse in yors to me, howe:
the dispensacion of the Lord itt is to have it
otherwise for the present, & therein I desire
to acquiesce, not being out of hope, but that
it may lye in his good pleasure in his time
to give us the mutuall comfort of or desires
the want whereof, he is able abundantly by
supply by his Staue pleme, wth indeed makes
all desires & is the comfort of all or comfo
& injoym.

4165 17

Salute yor deare Wife from me, bid her beware
of a Bondage spirit. feare is the naturall i[ssue]
of such a Spirit, the Antidote is love
The voyce of feare is (If I had donn
this,. If I had avoyded that how well
had been wth mee) I know this be
bcause her vaind reasoninge.

Love arguith on this wise: what
a Christ have I? what a ffather
and thorough him. what a Name
hath my ffather, Mercifull, gracio[us]
long suffering, abundant in goodnesse
truth, forgivingd iniquityd, transgress
and sins. what a Nature hath my
ffather, ther is love. what ffarre
p[ar]t, unchangiable, infinite. what a Coven
betweene Him and Christ, for all the Seed
for every one, wherein Hee undertakes all
the poore souls nothinge, The New coumant is grea
to, or upon the Soule, to wth it is passive and receiv

deal is known, but he can also prove elusive. Contemporary sources, not least his own letters and speeches, give profound insights into Cromwell during the 1640s and 1650s and allow us to come close to him in a way we cannot now approach many English or British monarchs of the second millennium AD. However, we know frustratingly little about his first forty years and even aspects of his later career, such as the precise religious forms he followed in his own worship, are poorly revealed in surviving sources. Some of his actions and policies are open to two different interpretations. For example, when during the Protectorate he had some of his political enemies removed to islands off the English mainland, was this the action of a cruel despot, subverting the judicial process and denying access to law and a fair trial, or those of a merciful humanitarian, allowing opponents a bearable life offshore rather than having them tried for treason with the likelihood of a capital sentence and a gruesome death? As we shall see, during the later 1640s and early 1650s Cromwell was lurking close to a string of rather shady actions – the army's seizure of the king in 1647, Charles's flight from captivity later that year, the military purge of parliament in 1648 and the resignation of the Nominated Assembly in 1653 – but on each occasion he claimed that he had no part in planning or bringing about these developments. Even modern historians broadly sympathetic towards Cromwell sometimes wonder whether his hands were quite so clean. Hero or villain, liberator or despot, Cromwell has continued to divide and puzzle historical opinion as he divided and puzzled many of his contemporaries. Academic and popular historians are drawn to this fascinating character time and again in an effort to get him right and comprehend how this obscure East Anglian farmer and minor landowner rose so far, so fast and with such profound consequences for his country in the middle years of the seventeenth century.

1

Early life 1599–1642

'I was by birth a gentleman; living neither in any considerable height, nor yet in obscurity' (from Cromwell's speech to his first Protectorate Parliament, September 1654)

Oliver Cromwell was born in Huntingdon in the Fenlands of East Anglia on 25 April 1599 and was baptised there in St John's church four days later. He was one of ten children of Robert Cromwell and Elizabeth, daughter of William Stewart. The couple had two other sons, but both died very young, and Cromwell became their only surviving son and heir. With his seven sisters, he grew up in the parental home in Huntingdon, and from 1610 to 1616 he attended the town's grammar school. In 1616 he went to Sidney Sussex College, Cambridge, but after his father's death he left university without a degree and spent much of the 1620s in Huntingdon. We know little more about his childhood and adolescence. In later letters and speeches Cromwell generally did not reflect on his early life or relate tales of his childhood. His comment in a speech of 1654, that he had been born into the landed class of gentry or gentlemen but that he came from the middling or lower reaches of that class, is one of his very few recorded comments on his background and early life and captures the ambiguity of his origins.

Cromwell was born into one of the greatest families of Huntingdonshire, major landowners whose fortunes had grown during the sixteenth century as they acquired considerable property, much of it church land sold after the Reformation. For a time the Cromwells were one of the ten richest families in Huntingdonshire and one of the hundred richest in East Anglia. Although they never obtained a hereditary title, for two successive generations the head of the family had been knighted – Sir Henry and his eldest son Sir Oliver – and several family members had served as JPs (Justices of the Peace, the county magistrates) and MPs (Members of Parliament, a term applied especially to members of the

Previous page: This portrait, by an unknown artist, is the only known image of Cromwell's father, Robert. In his will of 5 June 1617, he likened good health to 'a bubble of water' and noted that, being 'sick in body', 'by course of nature I cannot continue long in this world'. He was buried less than three weeks later.
The Cromwell Museum, Huntingdon

Elizabeth Cromwell, née Bourchier, married Cromwell in London in 1620 and gave birth to nine children between 1621 and 1638. This portrait, probably dating from the later 1640s or the 1650s, is attributed to Sir Peter Lely or one of his colleagues.
The Cromwell Museum, Huntingdon

elected House of Commons). Through marriage, the Cromwells were allied to many rich and powerful families, in East Anglia and beyond. But by the time Cromwell was born, the family's fortunes were turning, mainly because the then head of the family, Sir Oliver, spent too lavishly and exceeded his resources. By the opening decades of the seventeenth century the family was clearly in decline, selling land and property. Moreover Cromwell's own father, Robert, was a younger son of Sir Henry, one of ten children to survive into adulthood. Thus while the lion's share of Sir Henry's property had passed to his eldest son, Sir Oliver, the many younger sons and daughters had each received quite a modest settlement. Robert held a house in Huntingdon and other lands and properties in and around the town, an estate sufficient for him to be considered a gentleman, though in the lower reaches of the landed gentry.

After his father's death in 1617, Cromwell may have spent some time in London, though the suggestion that he attended one of the Inns of Court, the

The statue of Cromwell in St Ives, where he lived from 1631 to 1636, was designed by F.W. Pomeroy and unveiled in 1901, shortly after the tercentenary of Cromwell's birth. He is portrayed informally, striding forward, a large bible tucked under one arm.
Dr Peter Gaunt

legal training colleges, is unproven. By the early 1620s he had returned home to run the family estates and to look after his widowed mother and unmarried sisters. He brought to Huntingdon a wife, for in August 1620 he married in London Elizabeth Bourchier, eldest daughter of Sir James Bourchier, a successful London businessman who also had property in Essex. We do not know how the couple met or were introduced – perhaps mixing in Essex social circles, as Cromwell had kin in the county, or perhaps through an earlier family link, for in 1614 one of his wife's maternal aunts had wed one of Cromwell's uncles. The marriage proved long and happy and seven children were conceived between early 1621 and spring 1631, while the couple were living in Huntingdon. Cromwell inherited and ran the family estates around the town, perhaps renting out some land and probably overseeing various agriculturally related businesses. From the size of his inheritance and the value of the estate when almost all of it was sold, it is likely that during the 1620s Cromwell was making around £100 in a poor year, perhaps over £200 in a good year. Although in due course he held various offices in Huntingdon and represented the town in the parliament of 1628–29, his income and social standing were limited and insufficient for him to be appointed a JP for Huntingdonshire.

Cromwell's time in Huntingdon ended badly. Although evidence is meagre, he clearly supported the losing side in a power struggle in Huntingdon, a clash between different factions of leading townsmen which probably sprang from disagreements over how to spend a bequest to the town. In 1630 the victorious clique obtained a new royal charter permanently excluding from power their opponents, Cromwell included. Cromwell protested vigorously and, in consequence, was summoned before the Privy Council (the executive council of the British sovereign) and briefly imprisoned late in 1630. It is possible that this political crisis, in which Cromwell lost influence in his home town, was compounded by a social and economic crisis, a downturn in Cromwell's material standing, though the evidence for this is weaker. The wider family's links with the town had already loosened, for in the late 1620s Sir Oliver had sold his great house outside Huntingdon, and had moved away to a smaller, more rural property. In May 1631 Cromwell took a similar step, selling almost all his property in and around Huntingdon for £1800 and moving a few miles down the road to St Ives in Cambridgeshire, perhaps attracted there because an old friend had recently been appointed the town's vicar. He did not completely cut his ties, for he retained a small parcel of land and returned to Huntingdon for the baptism and burial of his last son, but his future lay elsewhere.

We know very little about the five years Cromwell spent at St Ives, from 1631 until 1636. He was apparently a tenant farmer, renting property from Henry Lawrence and earning his living from working the land. We do not know how much land he was renting, nor its precise location. Similarly, we have no idea how much rent Cromwell paid, nor the size of his income at this stage. Although renting land was not necessarily a social disgrace and some members of the elite rented parcels of land to supplement their own principal estates, Cromwell's move from being a freeholder to more or less exclusively a working tenant did mark a decline in his fortunes. He played some part in the affairs of St Ives, including the election of minor town officials, but his role was small. Another blow may have been the death of the couple's seventh child, a son James, probably conceived just a few weeks before they left Huntingdon, who was both baptised and buried in early January 1632. It is noticeable that no further children were born during the couple's years in St Ives. While it is tempting to speculate about deliberate contraception or suppressed libido during a period of material downturn, the evidence is inconclusive. Similarly, later stories that in the mid-1630s Cromwell was so disillusioned with his own fortunes, as well as with national affairs, that he contemplated emigration to the New World, are speculative and unproven, though others close to him, including his landlord, were involved around this time in establishing settlements in America and encouraging emigration.

In 1636 Cromwell's fortunes revived, not because of his own achievements but because he was the principal beneficiary of his maternal uncle, Sir Thomas Stewart of Ely, who died a childless widower in January 1636. Cromwell inherited not freehold land but a series of long leases on property and businesses, most of them in and around Ely. Almost all the property, including the timber-framed house near Holy Trinity church which became the Cromwells' home for the next few years, was leased from the Dean and Chapter of Ely cathedral. Cromwell's income was probably drawn from a number of sources, including sub-letting parts of his estate and overseeing agricultural and church businesses, especially tithe collecting in and around Ely. Together, they may have brought Cromwell around £300–400 annually, restoring him to the status and lifestyle of the gentry, albeit the lesser gentry. He began playing a role in the affairs of Ely, especially as trustee of one of the town's main charities. A surviving tax record of 1641 indicates that he was then amongst the twenty wealthiest inhabitants of Ely, hardly an exalted position, but probably a lot better than his fortunes at St Ives. Within weeks of

Cromwell and his family moved to this timber-framed house off St Mary's Street in Ely in 1636. Dating from the fifteenth century but with seventeenth-century additions and carefully restored in the late twentieth century, it is the only one of Cromwell's early homes that still stands.
East Cambridgeshire District Council

moving from St Ives, Cromwell's wife conceived their eighth child. The couple's last two children were born at Ely in the later 1630s.

The story of Cromwell's first forty years is conspicuously thin and the above account has been hedged with 'probably', 'perhaps' and 'may have'.

Strictly contemporary evidence, rather than lurid tales circulating long after 1640 when Cromwell had become famous and infamous, allows us to reconstruct the bare bones of his early life, but hardly provides a rounded picture. This is not surprising, nor perhaps much of a loss, for Cromwell passed his first four decades in obscurity, a minor East Anglian farmer earning a precarious living on or, for a time, perhaps below the lower rungs of the gentry. Like most of his peers at Huntingdon grammar school and Sidney Sussex College, his life was passing by beyond the glare of national events, a mixture of minor successes, failures and social fluctuations, a thinly documented life of no real historical importance. But because his life changed so utterly in the 1640s and 1650s and he became a figure of major national and international standing, historians pore over the meagre record in a sometimes desperate attempt to identify formative influences or discern the origins of traits which carried him to greatness.

Some historians have emphasised the feminine influence over Cromwell,

Cromwell was close to his mother, Elizabeth, portrayed here by an unknown artist, throughout her long life. She died in November 1654, in her ninetieth year, and was buried in Westminster Abbey, but at the Restoration her body was removed to a pit outside St Margaret's church, Westminster.
The Cromwell Museum, Huntingdon

the role of his widowed mother and many sisters, while others have suggested that Cromwell's character was shaped by the brooding fenland landscape in which he lived much of his life. Many look to more tangible insecurities, including ill-health, for there is some contemporary evidence that as young man he was prone to inflammation of the throat or chest and in autumn 1628 he consulted the most eminent London doctor of the day, who found him to be afflicted with coughing, excessive phlegm and digestive problems. More often, however, historians stress Cromwell's social and economic ambiguity and his mixed material fortunes in the 1620s and 1630s. Down to the early 1640s his income had probably never exceeded £400 per year and had often fallen well below that, he had lived in fairly small town houses rather than grander country seats, his holdings had been modest, generally in and around small towns and more often rented or leased than owned outright, and while he had held a few minor urban offices he had never served as a county JP, the real mark of gentility. Born into the lower levels of the gentry, his trajectory had been downwards, perhaps for a time slipping out of the gentry class, before being rescued by a bequest from a far more successful relative. On the other hand, his position in the junior branch of a great if declining family gave him potential or actual connections, albeit often rather distant, with some of the greatest families and most influential figures of the period. Again, although the evidence is frustratingly thin, there are indications that during the 1630s Cromwell had links with more senior social and political figures, some of whom were increasingly disillusioned with the drift of events.

Down to 1640 Cromwell does not come across as strongly political and his role in politics had been slight. He had been born during the closing years of Elizabeth I, though as she died in 1603 he cannot have had any personal recollection of her reign. His childhood and early manhood had passed during the reign of James I, the first Stuart king of England, who died in 1625, and he reached his prime during the reign of James' son and successor, Charles I. He cannot have been untouched by or unaware of the policies being pursued by James and Charles, not least the increased level of parliamentary and non-parliamentary taxes imposed during the 1620s, but his own involvement in the political and governmental processes had been limited. He had served in just one parliament, the third parliament of Charles I in 1628–29, but he was an inconspicuous MP whose one recorded speech was bland and muted. There is no sign that he criticised the policies of James or openly questioned, still less resisted, the rather more suspect ploys adopted by Charles, who reacted to parliamentary criticism of his financial, religious and foreign policies during the later 1620s by deciding to rule for the foreseeable future without calling further parliaments. From 1629 he dispensed with English parliaments, instead using his own prerogative and executive powers, together with the existing structures of church and local government, to advance his own policies, financed by a range of revived medieval sources of income. During the so-called Personal Rule of the 1630s Cromwell paid these non-parliamentary royal taxes and he was not one of the

'Oh, I lived in and loved darkness,
and hated the light. I was a chief,
the chief of sinners'

very small number of the elite who openly opposed the crown's financial and administrative innovations. On a more parochial stage, having had his fingers burnt in his native Huntingdon in 1630, his dabbling in urban administration thereafter had been at a much lower level. Although in the late 1630s he may have intervened in a local dispute relating to fen draining, he was probably seeking fair compensation for those with land rights affected by the scheme and was not opposing the policy as such or standing as champion of the common people.

On the other hand, there certainly was one formative experience in Cromwell's life which occurred before 1640 and was crucial in his later career. We know a little though not much about Cromwell's religious education and early beliefs. At school he probably fell under the influence of the schoolmaster, Dr Thomas Beard, a conformist whose faith was fairly conventional and drawn from the mainstream of the Jacobean Church of England. However, in later life Cromwell never referred to Beard, or to any other schoolmasters or university figures, as particularly influential in shaping his ideas. Religion lay at the root of the power struggle in Huntingdon, for the dispute apparently sprang from divisions over whether to spend part of a financial bequest on a new religious lectureship and over whom to appoint. Somewhere around that time, however, religion came to loom very large in Cromwell's life, for sometime in his twenties or thirties he underwent a conversion experience. In the fullest and most revealing of the mere handful of Cromwell's surviving letters which pre-date the civil war, he described in 1638 to Mrs St John how he had been living a sinful life, almost certainly exaggerating the blackness of his pre-conversion existence – 'Oh, I lived in and loved darkness, and hated the light. I was a chief, the chief of sinners. This is true; I hated godliness…'. Despite this, Cromwell felt that God had rescued him, shown him His divine mercy and chosen him for some special purpose – 'My soul is with the congregation of the firstborn, my body rests in hope, and if here I may honour my God either by doing or by suffering, I shall be most glad…The Lord accept me in His Son, and give me to walk in the light, and give us to walk in the light, as He is the light. He it is that enlighteneth our blackness, our darkness. I dare not say, He hideth His face from me. He giveth me to see light in His light. One beam in a dark place hath exceeding much refreshment in it: blessed be His Name for shining upon so dark a heart as mine!'

We do not know the nature of this conversion experience, whether it was a sudden flash linked to a particular event or a much longer process, nor exactly when it took place, though it had clearly occurred some time before October 1638, when he wrote to Mrs St John. Some historians place it around 1630–31, and link it to the events which ended Cromwell's years in Huntingdon, but this is largely speculative. Whenever it occurred, thereafter Cromwell fervently believed that God had picked him out for some special purpose and that in due course the Lord would reveal His intention to him and call upon him to work as one of His chosen servants.

Just as God did not fully reveal His intentions to Cromwell until the crises of the 1640s, so Cromwell's own religious beliefs are not fully revealed to historians until his surviving letters become far fuller after 1642. In due course, Cromwell came firmly to identify himself with the godly party, who believed that the church, religion and nation needed to be shaken up and that they had been charged by God to bring about such reformation. They sought further reform of the established state church, the Church of England, to eliminate what they saw as superfluous and superstitious Catholic practices which had survived the sixteenth-century Protestant Reformation and to create a simpler, lower, purer, more participatory church, with an emphasis on preaching and biblical interpretation;

'My soul is with the congregation of the firstborn, my body rests in hope, and if here I may honour my God either by doing or by suffering, I shall be most glad'

this would bring the word of God more directly and effectively to the people and would thus help to drive out sin and lead the people to more godly lives. Such objectives increasingly alienated this group from the religious policies of the king. From his accession in 1625, and with growing assurance during the Personal Rule, Charles sought not merely to entrench the power and position of the state church but also to drive through and enforce conformity to a whole series of changes designed to enhance the ceremonial and aesthetic aspects of religion, impose more rigid and ritualistic forms, emphasise the role of the minister as an intermediary between God and the people and ensure a greater separation between them, symbolised by the erection of permanent, railed-off altars at the east end of newly beautified churches. The overall effect of this policy, often labelled Arminianism, was to push the Church of England in a high church direction. The godly – after his conversion, Cromwell amongst them – were appalled by this approach, viewing it as at best an unnecessary and unwelcome tampering with the half-reformed Protestant church of Elizabeth and James and at worst an attempt to restore the dreaded and hated Roman Catholic faith by stealth.

Cromwell's religion informed the position he took in the parliaments Charles I called in 1640, the first to meet in England for eleven years. In both the brief and unproductive Short Parliament of the spring, and in the Long Parliament, which met from November onwards and which embarked upon a broad programme of reforming royal government, Cromwell sat as MP for Cambridge. Although he was not one of the leaders of parliamentary business and events, Cromwell did play a fairly active and prominent role in the opening two years of the Long Parliament, soon coming to attention as a forthright critic of royal policies. He was frequently named to committees, presented important petitions from individuals and communities, often carried messages and decisions from the Commons to the Lords and had a hand in the preparation or presentation of several important pieces of legislation, including bills to abolish episcopacy and guarantee annual parliaments. He was an early and strong supporter of proposals for parliament to appoint its own military commander and to do so by a parliamentary ordinance, rather than a full Act of Parliament, thereby removing the need to seek and obtain the royal assent. He also pressed for parliament to appoint guardians for the Prince of Wales, the heir to the throne, to safeguard his secular and religious upbringing and prevent undue Arminian or Catholic influence. He was outspoken in pressing for the prosecution of royalist supporters implicated in alleged plots against parliament and he repeatedly urged vigorous, armed responses not only to the major Irish Catholic rebellion against English Protestant rule which erupted in autumn 1641 but also to lesser Catholic conspiracies, real or imagined, at home and abroad. At times his inexperience, impetuosity and naivety showed, for some measures he supported were dropped or defeated and the angry or tactless outbursts to which he was prone proved counter-productive or earned him rebukes. Equally, he does not seem to have played much of a role in some of the major parliamentary developments of this period, such as the prosecution and removal of the king's chief minister, Sir Thomas Wentworth, Earl of Strafford, in spring 1641, or the presentation of a major list of alleged royal abuses, the Grand Remonstrance, in autumn 1641. Nonetheless, in the opening two years of the Long Parliament, Cromwell played a prominent and conspicuous role, surprisingly so for such an inexperienced figure. After all, when he took his seat in 1640 Cromwell had had little experience of politics or administration and his social standing was much weaker than most of the 500 or so MPs with whom he sat in the Commons.

Historians explain Cromwell's parliamentary role in 1640–42 in one of two

'That slovenly fellow which you see before us, who hath no ornament in his speech; I say that sloven, if we should ever come to have a breach with the King…in such case will be one of the greatest men of England'

A report of John Hampden's description of Cromwell, c.1641

ways. Some see him as a dynamic loner, driven forward by his religious conversion and his burning desire to do God's will and bring about reform. This gave him the confidence and energy to push himself onwards, overcoming inexperience, learning from his inevitable blunders and never flinching in the pursuit of the Lord's work. For these historians, Cromwell's record in 1640–42 is the first tangible sign of his rise from obscurity to fame and glory, essentially self-made, albeit backed by a burning faith and, as Cromwell would have put it, support from God. Others are unconvinced by the image of the self-made loner and instead speculate that he may have been acting as a front man for other, far more experienced and powerful politicians. Cromwell was allied by marriage, kinship or friendship to important and prominent critics of royal government in both Houses of the Long Parliament. These alliances, to which he may have owed his election for Cambridge in the first place, gave Cromwell a greater standing and potential role than his own political experience and social position would have bestowed. Some historians suggest that in 1640–42 Cromwell was employed by more powerful men to fly kites for them, to air policies and test the water for initiatives which might be pursued if they won sufficient support.

Whether self-made man or agent of others, Cromwell's star was clearly in the ascendant. Years later, in his memoirs, one MP recalled an exchange early in the Long Parliament, when Lord Digby asked John Hampden about the identity of an MP speaking in the House whom he did not recognise. Hampden replied that the 'slovenly fellow…who hath no ornament in his speech' was Cromwell and he supposedly added the prediction that, if it came to war, Cromwell would become 'one of the greatest men of England'. Born a gentleman he may have been, but down to 1640 Cromwell had lived largely in obscurity; in the early 1640s we catch the first glimpse of the considerable height which lay ahead.

2

The civil war 1642–46

'I was a person that, from my first employment, was suddenly preferred and lifted up from lesser trusts to greater; from my first being a captain of a troop of horse; and I did labour as well as I could to discharge my trust; and God blessed me as it pleased Him'
(from Cromwell's speech to a committee of his second Protectorate Parliament, April 1657)

For four years, between summer 1642 and summer 1646, Cromwell's life was dominated by the civil war. Firmly committed to the parliamentary cause and to waging and winning a war against royalist forces, he took up arms at the outset, and proved himself to be one of the most dynamic and successful officers of the war. His commitment, military talents and growing list of victories – as well as, Cromwell stressed, the support of God which made this possible – brought him rapid promotion, so that by 1644 he was second-in-command of parliament's largest regional army and by 1645 of parliament's main national army. He played a significant role first in turning the tide of the conflict and then in securing complete and unconditional military victory. He campaigned extensively in many regions of England, covering perhaps 2000 miles or more, and took part in dozens of battles, skirmishes and sieges. Inevitably, therefore, he was far more soldier than politician during these years, though he remained an MP and returned occasionally to London and to parliament, especially during winter when active campaigning waned. Although he probably sat in the Commons for a total of barely twenty weeks between August 1642 and June 1646, his growing military reputation enhanced his political standing – on a brief return to parliament late in the war he was reportedly 'looked on as a wonder' by fellow MPs as he passed through Westminster Hall – and provided the power-base for the resumed political career which followed.

Previous page: In July 1643 Cromwell
attacked royalist troops taking refuge
in Burghley House, the Elizabethan
mansion outside Stamford. According
to the newspapers, the assault was 'a
difficult task and full of danger', but at
length the defenders' 'Spirits began to
fail them' and they surrendered.
English Heritage Photographic Library

In 1640–41, during the opening year of the Long Parliament, Charles I had
made a string of concessions, in the face of overwhelming parliamentary criticism
abandoning the policies and personnel of the Personal Rule. In the process, a
growing proportion of the political nation had come round to support Charles,
believing that he had firmly abandoned the unwelcome political, financial and
religious innovations which had marked his reign down to 1640 and feeling that
he could now be trusted with church and state and that to push ahead with
further reforms would destabilise the constitution. Strengthened by this growing
support, an embryonic royalist party, by 1641–42 Charles was deliberately
portraying himself as the defender of the traditional church and state and firmly
resisting demands that he concede more royal authority. However, many other
politicians felt that they should press on further to limit the military and political
powers of the king and to create a purer church, in part because they genuinely
believed that additional reforms were necessary to avoid another crisis, in part
because they suspected that Charles's concessions of 1640–41 were insincere and
made only under duress and that if the reform programme stalled at that point
Charles would retain sufficient power to reverse them. Thus they pushed on
with their reforms, trying to whittle down the military and executive powers
of the crown, perhaps with parliament commanding the army and appointing
governmental officials, and to reform the Church of England, perhaps by
abolishing the episcopal system and ending the authority of bishops and
archbishops appointed by the crown. They continued to take this line, even
though the divisions within parliament, the political elite and the whole
nation were widening dangerously. By the opening months of 1642, as the
king quit London and began calling his supporters to him and arming them,
there was clearly a risk that these constitutional, political and religious differences

could spill over into armed conflict and civil war between king and parliament.

Cromwell was one of those MPs who were not won over by the king's concessions but who firmly and consistently supported the continuing reform programme. Despite – or perhaps because of – his lack of prior military experience, he seemed far from squeamish in 1641–42 about the possibility of armed conflict, voicing strong support for firm and potentially military responses to a string of crises. So it is not surprising that in summer 1642, as both king and parliament were raising troops in England and Wales, jockeying for position and trying to secure key ports, towns and other territories, but before the war proper had begun, Cromwell was one of the first MPs to take physical action in the unfolding English conflict. Determined to prevent the wealthy Cambridge colleges sending their silver to the king at York to help fund his imminent war effort, in early August Cromwell left London and made for his constituency. Gathering armed supporters either en route or around Cambridge, Cromwell succeeded in turning back or preventing from leaving the town much of the silver which the colleges intended for the king, at the same time ensuring that the town's supply of arms was secured for parliament's use. Cromwell was by no means the only committed parliamentarian or MP to employ direct, military-backed force in support of the parliamentary cause in summer 1642, but at this stage, before the king had formally declared war – he raised his standard at Nottingham on 22 August – only a very small minority were prepared to go this far. By intervening and seizing private property without clear orders when the country was still formally at peace, Cromwell was placing himself in an exposed position.

In the event, the king declared war soon after, and during autumn 1642 both sides not only intensified their efforts to secure resources but also deployed

Opposite: The principal towns and other sites where Cromwell was based or campaigned during the civil war, 1642–46. During the civil war Cromwell campaigned mainly in the East Midlands, East Anglia, central southern England and the south-west. He did not campaign in Wales and the Marches and very rarely travelled north and west of a line linking the Severn and the Humber.

their growing armies. Commissioned a captain, Cromwell seems to have spent early autumn not in parliament but in his home area, raising for parliament a troop of horse (about sixty mounted soldiers) and working to strengthen parliament's hold over Cambridge. In October he and his troop rendezvoused with the main parliamentary army, commanded by the Earl of Essex, which was shadowing the king in the West Midlands. He arrived too late to take part in the main engagement at Edgehill, Warwickshire, on 23 October, but he was probably present late in the day and witnessed or participated in the fragmented closing stages of that battle. He and his men then probably remained with Essex's army both as it marched back to London and when it made a stand at Turnham Green to the west of the capital on 13 November, in a show of force which blocked Charles's advance on London and persuaded the king to fall back. The civil war was not decided by a single decisive campaign in autumn 1642 and instead both sides regrouped and dug in during the winter, the king at his new headquarters in Oxford, parliament in London, to prepare for renewed fighting.

The indecisive outcome of the Edgehill campaign changed the nature of the civil war, for thereafter it became a rather dour and inevitably protracted territorial conflict. From late 1642 onwards, both sides focused their efforts on carving up England and Wales, securing and holding blocks of territory, urban and rural, by stationing bodies of troops and administrators there, and then regularly tapping the resources of those areas – men, money, horses, food, materials and so forth – to supply and maintain a long-term war effort. King and parliament generally maintained and deployed one or more principal armies during the main campaigning seasons, from spring to autumn, but other troops served at a local or regional level, in smaller provincial armies or in the hundreds of royalist and parliamentary garrisons through which territory was controlled.

This process was underway during winter 1642–43 and by spring 1643 most of England and Wales had been secured by one side or the other. The king initially held northern England, almost the whole of Wales, most of the area along the English–Welsh border, the far south-west of England (Cornwall) and a tongue of territory from the Welsh borders across the West Midlands to Oxfordshire. Parliament held the rest of England – much of the central and East Midlands, East Anglia, where Cromwell was already active, southern England and the south-east – and the far south-west of Wales (Pembrokeshire).

At the beginning of 1643 Cromwell was promoted to colonel with command of a cavalry regiment within one of parliament's regional armies, that of the Eastern Association, based in East Anglia and the East Midlands. Between January 1643 and January 1644 Cromwell was on almost continuous active service there, struggling to resist the rising tide of royalism – 1643 proved to be a very good year for the king's forces, who advanced and overran many areas initially secured by parliament – and meeting the threat of the king's northern army which was overwhelming Lincolnshire and menacing the parliamentary heartlands of East Anglia and the East Midlands. In March Cromwell toured towns in Suffolk and Norfolk, ensuring that they were loyal to parliament and quickly extinguishing a pro-royalist rising in Lowestoft. At the end of the summer he was present at a larger operation against a far more significant royalist rising in King's Lynn. During the opening quarter of the year he spent much of his time at Cambridge and Huntingdon, working to strengthen the parliamentary hold over them and converting them into viable centres of operations in the surrounding areas. In the process he bolstered the north-western frontier of East Anglia by cementing parliament's hold on the valley of the Great Ouse and the main towns flanking it. In late April and early May he pushed forward to secure a more advanced north-western front along the Nene valley, strengthening parliament's hold over Peterborough and, following a very brief siege, crushing a band of royalist soldiers and civilians in Crowland or Croyland, eight miles north-east of Peterborough; in mid-July, an even briefer siege saw Cromwell overwhelm royalist troops who had taken refuge in Burghley House, a similar distance north-west of Peterborough. From mid-May onwards Cromwell also made frequent incursions deep into Lincolnshire, generally working with others in combined operations against the advancing royalists. Thus in May Cromwell helped first to recapture Grantham and then repulse a body of royalists in a brief engagement at Belton, north of the town, and several times during May and June and again in late November he was part of a combined parliamentary army which, though never strong enough directly to attack Newark, approached and harried the major royalist base. In late July he jointly led a relieving force which engaged and repulsed a royalist army outside Gainsborough, though he had to abandon the town and fall back to Lincoln when the main royalist army approached. Not until the autumn did Cromwell take part in a really important and decisive field engagement, when on 11 October he was one of the principal commanders of the parliamentary forces which defeated a large royalist army at Winceby, near Horncastle, thereby effectively halting the royalist advance through Lincolnshire.

Cromwell's military record during 1643 was sound enough. He comes across as an inexperienced but keen regional commander whose achievements began to win him national attention, a rising star of the parliamentary cause and one of the few parliamentary officers to achieve significant military success in a year generally marked by royalist victories. In part, that success can be ascribed to Cromwell's own qualities, including his commitment, enthusiasm and hard work, his ability to learn quickly and his willingness to operate on his own initiative as well as with others. But it also owed something to luck. Many of the more senior Eastern Association commanders were called away to fight elsewhere during 1643, leaving Cromwell largely undisturbed to organise the defence of his home area, operating with short supply lines and drawing on the resources of a fairly solid parliamentarian region. He encountered royalist forces who were fighting a long way from their northern heartlands and whose drive south was running out of steam as their supply lines became stretched and their forces divided, with much of the army diverted to a long and futile siege of Hull. Had Cromwell been a regional commander operating in less favourable circumstances, perhaps in Wiltshire or Dorset, facing the united and well-supplied royalist armies roaring across south-western and southern England, his military record in 1643 may well have been very different.

Cromwell's letters of 1643 reveal a number of traits which coloured his later career. Firstly, he rapidly acquired confidence in his own command. At Belton he appeared hesitant, holding his troops to await a royalist attack before at length consulting his fellow-officers and reaching a joint decision that they should charge the enemy. Two and a half months later, at Gainsborough, Cromwell was far more decisive, showing little hesitation in committing his cavalry to charging the royalist position, even though that meant attacking up hill and over rough ground. At Gainsborough, too, we see signs of what became a feature of Cromwell's approach to battle, for he strove to maintain tight control over his men, particularly his cavalry, retaining a reserve of horse in good order to counter any royalist reserve and ensure that an enemy army, once collapsing, would be unable to make a stand or launch a counter-attack.

Secondly, we catch our first glimpse of Cromwell's belief that God was shaping military events and giving him victories. Thus of Belton he wrote that 'God hath given us, this evening, a glorious victory' for 'by God's providence they [the royalists] were immediately routed', while his correspondence describing his victory outside Gainsborough and his subsequent orderly retreat to Lincoln are full of phrases such as 'it hath pleased God to favour us', 'it's great evidence of God's favour' and 'it hath pleased the Lord to give your servant and soldiers a notable victory'. Some colleagues in Suffolk were advised that God was saying 'Up and be doing, and I will help you and stand by you', Cromwell adding that 'there is nothing to be feared but our own sin and sloth'.

Thirdly, Cromwell was unusually concerned about his troops, pushing for them to be well paid, fed and equipped, and he took a keen interest in the administrative, material and financial mechanisms which underpinned the war effort. But his concerns went much further. He wanted his troops to be well

'I had rather have a plain russet-coated captain that knows what he fights for, and loves what he knows, than that which you call a gentleman and is nothing else. I honour a gentleman that is so indeed'

disciplined both on and off the battlefield, of good moral and spiritual standing and fully committed to the righteous and godly cause for which they were fighting. Thus several times during 1643, as well as later in the war, Cromwell argued that parliament should be selective in recruitment, seeking 'such men as had the fear of God before them, and [who] made some conscience of what they did'. He hoped to find them amongst the upper echelons of society but he came to recognise that parliament could not recruit sufficient troops from that social band alone and so accepted that less elevated, 'plain' men would have to be recruited, though they must be honest and sober, 'patient of wants, faithful and conscientious in the employment'. It was in this context that Cromwell famously wrote in 1643, 'I had rather have a plain russet-coated captain that knows what he fights for, and loves what he knows, than that which you call a gentleman and is nothing else. I honour a gentleman that is so indeed'. Cromwell was no social revolutionary and was not arguing here that those below gentry level were better than gentlemen – indeed, committed and godly gentlemen made the best soldiers, Cromwell wrote. But the pressing need to find sufficient committed and properly motivated men led him to recruit from lower down the social scale and to advise others to do so too. Cromwell was well aware that his promotion of non-gentlemen might make him vulnerable to accusations of undermining the social order – 'it may be it provokes some spirits to see such plain men made captains of horse', he wrote in 1643 – just as his willingness to recruit religiously motivated figures holding a variety of Protestant beliefs might lead to claims that he was undermining the church and encouraging heresy.

Fourthly, during 1643 Cromwell became acutely aware that not all parliamentarians were as strongly committed as he was to waging and winning the war. He was frustrated by what he saw as the foot-dragging of civilian administrators in several East Anglian counties, exasperated by their unwillingness to grasp the urgent situation and meet the imminent danger of royalist invasion, and outspoken in condemning their slow and patchy response to requests for money and recruits. In May he wrote to the mayor and corporation of Colchester 'Judge you the danger of neglect, and how inconvenient this improvidence, or unthrifty, may be to you!', in June he advised the Cambridge commissioners 'This is not a time to pick and choose for pleasure. Service must be done. Command you, and be obeyed!', while in August he implored them to 'Raise all your bands;…get up what volunteers you can;…I beseech you spare not, but be expeditious and industrious…You must act lively; do it without distraction'. Equally critical of senior military commanders, in May he wrote to the Lincolnshire commissioners, scathingly condemning Lord Grey for staying at home to protect Leicester rather than rendezvousing with him in Lincolnshire, and pledging to 'deal as freely with him when I meet him as you can desire'. Cromwell returned to parliament in January 1644 in part to support an attack on another lacklustre commander, Lord Willoughby, who was soon removed, as well as to press for improvements to the Eastern Association.

Cromwell's return to parliament early in 1644 was brief and coincided with two promotions. In February he was appointed to parliament's main executive committee, the Committee of Both Kingdoms, and around that time he was promoted to lieutenant-general of the horse in the Eastern Association army, thus becoming its second-in-command under the Earl of Manchester. By the beginning of March he had left London and he spent the next nine months on active service, campaigning now over a wider geographical area. In early March and again during the autumn he led short campaigns in the western Home Counties, harrying royalist bases in Berkshire, Buckinghamshire and Oxfordshire, while from mid-March to mid-April and again in early September he was back in his home area, bolstering the defences of Cambridge and Huntingdon. However, for much of the year he was with Manchester and the Eastern Association army as it marched north in early May to join a huge Anglo-Scottish parliamentary force besieging the king's northern capital of York, while in October he was part of a combined force which threatened the king's position in the south Midlands. Both operations culminated in major battles in which Cromwell played a prominent role.

Cromwell's greatest military success during 1644 was his role at Marston Moor on 2 July, the biggest battle of the English civil war and one of the most decisive. To rescue his besieged northern capital, threatened from the south by English parliamentary forces and from the north by a Scottish army which entered the war to support the English parliament, the king dispatched a large relieving army led by Prince Rupert, who engaged the Anglo-Scottish parliamentary army on rolling moorland to the west of York. Cromwell, in overall command of the cavalry on the left wing of the parliamentary line, played a crucial role, for his cavalry carried all before it, broke the opposing royalist horse and then retained sufficient shape and discipline to swing round and begin tearing into the now exposed flank of the enemy infantry, securing an over-whelming victory. In the wake of the battle, northern royalism collapsed and in due course almost the whole of northern England was secured by parliament. Three days after the battle, Cromwell wrote in euphoric tones of 'this great victory given unto us, such as the like never was since this war began. It had all the evidences of an absolute victory obtained by the Lord's blessing upon the godly party principally. We never charged but we routed the enemy...God made them as stubble to our swords...Give glory, all the glory, to God'. But in this letter, one of the most famous and moving of the civil war, Cromwell also had to convey bad news to its recipient, his brother-in-law Valentine Walton, for his eldest son had perished on the battlefield. 'It's our duty to sympathise in all mercies; that we may praise the Lord together in chastisements or trials, that so we may sorrow together', Cromwell cautioned at the outset. A little later he revealed to Walton that 'God hath taken away your eldest son by a cannon-shot. It brake his leg. We were necessitated to have it cut off, whereof he died'. He sought to comfort Walton with the thought that his son was a godly young man, who had died in a godly cause and who was now with the Lord. 'There is your precious child full of glory, to know sin nor sorrow any more. He was a gallant young man, exceeding precious...fit for God. You have cause to bless the Lord. He is a glorious saint in Heaven, wherein you ought exceedingly to rejoice...You may do all things by the strength of Christ. Seek that, and you shall easily bear your trial'.

However, all did not run smoothly for Cromwell during 1644. His service at the siege of York during the spring, culminating at Marston Moor, brought him into close contact with the Scottish army, since autumn 1643 military allies of the English parliament. He did not like the narrow religious outlook he found in many Scottish commanders, especially their ambition for a Presbyterian-style religious settlement in England and Wales once the war was won. Cromwell had no quarrel with Presbyterianism as such, but by 1644 he clearly welcomed the plurality of Protestant faiths springing up in England and Wales and opposed the possible reimposition of any single church. His relaxed and tolerant religious attitude, his opinion that 'the State, in choosing men to serve them', should take 'no notice of their opinions; if they be willing faithfully to serve them, that satisfies', and his strong support for a Baptist junior officer whom a senior officer was seeking to dismiss, brought him into conflict with Scots who were pursuing

a Presbyterian settlement as well as with English commanders sympathetic to it. Moreover, Cromwell became disenchanted with the leadership of his immediate superior, the Earl of Manchester. In Cromwell's eyes, Manchester appeared half-hearted about the war, hesitant at pushing for full military victory, apparently in favour of a compromise peace with the king and thus prone to inactivity. For example, during the two months immediately following Marston Moor, the Earl moved very slowly through Yorkshire and the fringes of Lincolnshire, rarely engaging the enemy and achieving little. But Cromwell's own military record during 1644 was not above question. He was part of a large combined army which, by threatening royalist bases in the south Midlands during the autumn, forced the king to give battle. But at the second Battle of Newbury on 27 October the parliamentarians adopted a complex strategy, dividing their army into two; the commanding officers did not coordinate their attacks and Cromwell himself appeared strangely indecisive, failing to follow up an assault by one of his colleagues. For Cromwell, the inability of parliamentary forces to push home their numerical advantage at Newbury reinforced his view that several colleagues, including Manchester, had neither ability nor stomach to win the war. But to others, Cromwell seemed at fault at and after Newbury, failing to cooperate with colleagues or obey orders, perhaps unwilling to push for a victory which might lead to a religious settlement he opposed.

Against this background, Cromwell, who returned to London in November, quickly launched a stinging and wide-ranging attack on Manchester in parliament, repeatedly and in detail denouncing him for military failings during 1644 and alleging that the Earl wished to see the war ended by a compromise peace, not by military victory. But Manchester was far from overwhelmed, and from the Lords he launched vigorous counter-attacks, pointing to Cromwell's own military shortcomings, and accusing him of anti-Scottish and anti-Presbyterian prejudices and of favouring fanatics, heresy and social instability. It is a measure of Cromwell's growing political experience and maturity, as well as of his enhanced stature and support, that in December he was able to change tack very effectively and both neutralise Manchester and help realign key military policies. In one or more major parliamentary speeches on 9 December Cromwell dropped his attack on Manchester, acknowledging that everyone, including himself, had made mistakes during the campaign. He combined this with a proposal, probably formulated by others, that all members of parliament who held military command should lay down their commissions, so ensuring that the war would henceforth be pursued more vigorously by full-time military commanders and that campaigning could not be sidetracked by political differences. In what was clearly a well-planned and coordinated manoeuvre, others supported this idea and during the opening weeks of 1645 Cromwell worked with parliamentary colleagues to convert it into a binding, legislative format, the Self-Denying Ordinance. At the same time parliament voted to reorganise its armies, combining several regional forces, including the Eastern Association army, with fresh recruits to form a large, more effective national army, dubbed the New Model Army,

Sir Thomas Fairfax became parliament's Lord General and Cromwell's immediate commander in spring 1645. He is shown on horseback, while in the background a civil war army moves forward, the men arranged in distinct blocks of musketeers, pikemen and cavalry. From J. Sprigge, *Anglia Rediviva*, 1647. *The British Library, 9512, f.7*

which it was hoped would engage and defeat the main royalist forces and break the king's continuing hold over much of the Midlands and southern England.

Cromwell briefly returned to the field in early spring, campaigning in southern England and around Oxfordshire during March and April, in what should have been the swansong of his military career. As MP for Cambridge, he was bound by the Self-Denying Ordinance to resign his commission by mid-May. However, by that time the king's main army was threatening to wreak havoc in the Midlands, and parliament voted to extend Cromwell's commission for a further forty days. In early June the new parliamentary commander-in-chief, Sir Thomas Fairfax, requested Cromwell's appointment as lieutenant-general of the horse and second-in-command of the New Model Army, and parliament complied. Thereafter, parliament repeatedly extended Cromwell's military command. Those keen to portray Cromwell as a devious manipulator see dark plots in this. They suggest that his promotion or strong support of the Self-Denying Ordinance was a means to remove Manchester and other opponents via a circuitous route rather than directly attacking them in a way which allowed them to defend themselves, and that from the outset Cromwell and his cronies planned to exempt Cromwell from the ordinance's provisions. Certainly, the end result was to remove from military

command not only Manchester but also other members of the Lords and Commons whose approach to the war and views on possible future political and religious settlements differed from his own. In their place, Cromwell gained promotion and was now working alongside military colleagues more in tune with him. But there is no clear evidence to support the conspiracy theory. The original ordinance, which Cromwell backed, did not provide for any exemptions and an early attempt to exempt the then commander-in-chief, Essex, was voted down. Although the question of exempting individuals remained in the air, thereafter it seemed unlikely that anyone would evade the ordinance and not until very late in proceedings, after Cromwell had left London and was on campaign, was such provision added.

From May 1645 until June 1646 Cromwell was again almost permanently on campaign. For much of the period he was campaigning with Fairfax and the New Model Army, initially to meet the threat of the king's army in the Midlands, bringing Charles to battle and crushing his forces at Naseby in Northamptonshire on 14 June, and then on a lengthy operation to mop up remaining royalist regional armies and garrisons in the south-west. During late summer 1645 Cromwell accompanied Fairfax as they crushed a western army at Langport in Somerset and captured Bridgwater, Bristol, Sherborne castle and an array of lesser royalist bases in Wiltshire, Somerset and Dorset. During early autumn Cromwell commanded part of the New Model Army on a separate campaign to wrap up a handful of royalist strongholds in central southern England, including Devizes in Wiltshire and Winchester and Basing House in Hampshire. He rejoined Fairfax and the main army in late October and spent the winter on campaign in eastern Devon. The opening months of 1646 saw Cromwell and Fairfax securing the far south-west, capturing Exeter, Launceston and other towns, defeating royalist forces in small engagements at Bovey Tracey and Torrington and accepting the surrender of the king's Cornish army near Truro in late March. Cromwell was present during May and June at the siege of Oxford, the king's capital, which concluded in mid-summer when Charles surrendered and ordered his few remaining garrisons to lay down their arms.

The closing phase of the war underlined Cromwell's growing abilities and beliefs. At Naseby and elsewhere, he retained tight control over his men, especially the cavalry, to ensure that they remained in good order, effective in winning an engagement but also thereby sparing unnecessary bloodshed. Similarly, wherever possible he accepted the surrender of a besieged stronghold on reasonable terms and maintained discipline as it was handed over. A glaring exception was his capture in October 1645 of Basing House, where Cromwell brushed aside attempts by the royalists to negotiate and instead unleashed a heavy artillery bombardment and then a brutal storming which saw the stronghold fall, many defenders put to the sword and the house first plundered and then torched.

The massively fortified mansion at Basing, repeatedly besieged by parliament during the war, comprised medieval buildings on the site of a castle, collectively known as the 'old house', and a grand Tudor mansion or 'new house', all enclosed by a ditch and a curtain wall with towers.
British Museum

Opposite: Cromwell's letter to the Speaker, describing the successful bombardment and storming of Basing, revealed that his men had refused the royalists' request for 'a parley' and had put many of them 'to the sword' and that the house had been 'exceedingly ruined'.
From *Perfect Diurnall of Some Passages in Parliament, and from Other Parts of the Kingdome*, 13–20 October 1645.
The British Library, E266 (5)

A. THE OLDE HOVSE . B. THE NEW. C. THE TOWER THAT IS HALFE BATTERED DOVNE. D. THE KINGES BREAST WORKS. E. THE PARLIAMENTS BREAST WORKS.

This uncharacteristically severe approach may well reflect Cromwell's religious prejudices, for though tolerant of Protestant beliefs he hated Roman Catholicism, and it was known that Basing House was not only owned by a Catholic but also served as a haven for Catholic royalists, 'a nest of Romanists', as Cromwell reportedly called it.

The string of victories of 1645–46 confirmed to Cromwell that he was doing God's will and that the Lord was shaping events. Naseby was 'none other than the hand of God, and to Him alone belongs the victory', Langport caused Cromwell to exclaim 'Now can we give all the glory to God, and desire all may do so, for it is all due unto Him!', and the capture of Bristol was 'none other than the work of God...he must be a very Atheist that doth not acknowledge it'. Writing a month or so after Naseby, Cromwell recalled that 'when I saw the enemy drawn up and march in gallant order towards us, and we a company of poor ignorant men...I could not...but smile out to God in praises, in assurance of victory, because God would, by things that are not, bring to naught things that

SIR,

I Thanke God, I can give you a good account of *Bazing*. After our batteries placed, we setled the severall posts for the storme; Col. Dalbeere was to be on the North side of the use neere the Grange, Col. Pickering on his left hand, and Sir Hardresse Wallers and Col. Mountagues Regiments next him; We stormed this morning after six of the clocke, the gnall for falling on was the firing foure of our Canon, which being done, our men fell on with reat resolution and cheerefunesse, we tooke the two houses without any considerable losse to ur selves; Col. Pickering stormed the new house, passed through, and got the gate of the old House, whereupon they summoned a parley, which our men would not heare, in the meane ime Col. Mountagues, and Sir Hardresse Wallers Regiments assaulted the strongest worke, where the enemy kept his Court of guard, which with great resolution they recovered, eating the enemy from a whole Culverin, and from that worke, which having done, they drew heir Ladders after them, and got over another Worke, and the house wall before they could nter. In this Sir Hardresse Waller performing his duty with honour and diligence, was sh t n the arme, but not dangerous, we have had little losse, many of the enemy our men put to he Sword, and some Officers of quality, most of the rest we have prisoners, amongst which he Marquesse, and Sir Robert Peake, with divers other Officers, whom I have ordered to e sent up to you. We have taken about ten pieces of Ordnance, with much Ammunition, and ur Souldiers a good encouragement. I humbly offer to you to have this place utterly slighted for these following reasons: It will aske about 800 men to mannage it, it is no Frontier, he Countrey is poore about it, the place exceedingly ruined by our batteries and mortar-pieces, and a fire which fell upon the place since our taking it. If you please to take the Garrison at Farnham, some out of Chichester, and a good part of the foot which were here under Dalbeer, and make a strong quarter at Newbery, with three or four Troops of horse, I dare be confident it would not onely be a curbe to Denington but a security, and a frontier to all these parts, in as much as Newbery lies upon the River, and will prevent any incursion from Dennington, Wallingford or Farringdon, into these parts, and by lying there, will make the trade most secure between Bristol and London for all Carriages. And I believe the Gentlemen of Sussex and Hampshire will with more chearfulnesse contribute, to maintaine a Garrison on a Frontier, then in their Bowels which will have lesse safety in it, Sir I hope not to delay, but march towards the West to morrow: and to be as diligent as I may in my expedition thither, I must speake my judgement to you, that if you intend to have your worke carried on, Recruits of foot must be had, and a course taken to pay your army, else believe me Sir, it may not be able to answer the worke you have for it to do. I entreated Col. Hammon to waite upon you, who was taken by a mistake whilst we lay before this Garrison, whom God safely delivered to us to our great joy, but to his losse of almost all he had, which the enemy tooke from him. The Lord grant that these mercies may be acknowledged with all thankefulnesse. God exceedingly abounds in his goodnesse to us, and will not be weary untill righteousnesse and peace meet: and that he hath brought forth a glorious worke for the happinesse of this poore Kingdome, wherein desires to serve God and you, with a faithfull hand,

Basingstoke, 14 Octob. 1645.

          Your most humble servant,
          OLIVER CRUMWELL

are. Of which I had great assurance; and God did it'. But by 1645–46 Cromwell's mind was also turning to the post-war settlement and he began to prompt parliament about the religious arrangements which God and the army favoured. After Naseby he advised the Speaker of the Commons to reward the parliamentary troops by securing their liberties, especially religious liberties – 'He that ventures his life for the liberty of his country, I wish he trust God for the liberty of his conscience, and you for the liberty he fights for'. Arguing even more strongly for religious liberty, after the capture of Bristol he advised the Speaker – 'Presbyterians, Independents, all had here the same spirit of faith and prayer; the same pretence and answer; they agree here, know no names of difference: pity it is should be otherwise anywhere. All that believe, have the real unity, which is most glorious, because inward and spiritual, in the Body, and to the Head. As for being united in forms, commonly called Uniformity, every Christian will for peace-sake study and do, as far as conscience will permit; and from brethren, in things of the mind we look for no compulsion, but that of light and reason'.

That the House of Commons censored and omitted these demands for religious liberty when they published Cromwell's dispatches was a sign that all was not well and pointed to further, looming conflicts. By summer 1646 Cromwell's civil war was over, ending in complete military victory, secured in no small part by his own actions and dynamism. His stature hugely strengthened by his civil war record, he now possessed potentially extensive if still largely untested political power and parliamentary influence. As the guns fell silent, there lay ahead – for Cromwell, as for his political and military allies – other potentially bitter battles, to be fought over the shape of the peace and the religious and political settlement of the shattered nation.

By the end of the war Cromwell was one of the most prominent parliamentary generals, ranked alongside the Earls of Manchester and Essex, and Lord Fairfax, whose military careers had ended by 1646, as well as Sir Thomas Fairfax who would work with Cromwell in the later 1640s.
Ashmolean Museum

3

The failure of settlement 1646–49

'I have lived the latter part of my life in, if I may say so, the fire, in the midst of trouble' (from Cromwell's speech to a committee of his second Protectorate Parliament, March 1657)

From summer 1646 Cromwell sought to help rebuild the nation, his words and actions pointing to his principal goals – to ensure that parliament and its army worked together in harmony to produce a stable settlement which would secure liberties but also safeguard the tenets of the traditional constitution, so that England and Wales would never again be torn apart by civil war. Although these broad goals were shared by most participants on the parliamentary side, by 1646 there was emerging a range of individuals and factions with their own particular preferences and agenda, many of them very different from those of Cromwell and his immediate colleagues. Accordingly, the post-war years were marked by disputes and power-struggles between key players on the parliamentary side. As a senior army officer and prominent politician, Cromwell was intimately involved in these power-struggles, was often in the midst of trouble and fire, sometimes seizing the initiative, more often buffeted by others or forced into uncomfortable positions. It was not a happy experience, and Cromwell fell prey to periods of foreboding and gloom as the clarity of fighting a civil war, the succession of crisp, decisive military victories and the apparent parliamentary unity of the war years gave way to something far more messy and intractable. Moreover, in many ways the years 1646–49 saw the failure of most of Cromwell's goals. Far from working together in harmony, parliament became irreparably divided and the dominant parliamentary group turned against the parliamentary army. Despite Cromwell's strong misgivings, the army reacted by involving itself in the political process and became wracked by internal divisions. Instead of banishing the spectre of civil

Previous page: In the mid-1640s,
Cromwell probably viewed elected
parliaments as central to any
settlement. This contemporary image
of the House of Commons in session
shows the Speaker seated on a large
chair and around him, on tiered
benches, many of the 500 or so MPs.
British Museum, Dunbar medal

war, by 1648 the peace-making process had collapsed and England and Wales
were torn apart by renewed war. The period closed with military intervention
in government which swept away the traditional constitution. By 1648–49 wider
developments had forced Cromwell to support or acquiesce in radical policies
which would have been unthinkable to him in 1646, let alone in 1642.

By 1646 Cromwell had clear views on the future religious settlement.
He accepted the fragmentation of the Protestant church during the war and
the appearance amongst soldiers and civilians of several new Protestant faiths,
practices and sects. He believed that this was God's will and that each faith
contained an element of God's truth. Thus in Cromwell's eyes it was essential
that freedom for various Protestant faiths to practise be continued and guaranteed,
with any religious settlement enshrining the principle of religious liberty or,
as Cromwell usually phrased it, 'liberty of conscience' for different brands of
Protestantism. As Cromwell later noted, religious liberty 'was not the thing at
first contested for, but God brought it to that issue at last' and it was 'the peculiar
interest all this while contended for'. By the mid-1640s, the pursuit of religious
liberty had become a central tenet of Cromwell's approach and thereafter he
consistently saw it as the centrepiece of any new form of government. He was
implacably opposed to any settlement which might restrict or remove religious
liberty or envisaged the restoration of a single state church to which everyone
must conform. On the other hand, Cromwell's political preferences in the
immediate post-war period do not emerge so clearly in his letters and speeches
and were probably not as strongly formed by 1646. He seems to have envisaged
that a settlement would be reached with Charles I, retaining an active monarch
at the head of state, though he probably favoured effective new restrictions on
the crown's executive and prerogative powers. Beyond that, he probably wished

to see the restoration of large elements of the pre-war constitution, complete with traditional civilian government via a succession of elected parliaments. However, much of Cromwell's political programme did not emerge clearly until the later 1640s.

Cromwell was back in London by early July 1646 and soon moved his family – wife, widowed mother and several children – from Ely to a house he acquired there. For the remainder of the year and into 1647 he attended parliament regularly. Within the Commons he was allied to and in sympathy with one of the two main factions which emerged post-war, the so-called Independents, who favoured a religious settlement based upon liberty of conscience, and a political and constitutional settlement based upon tight new restrictions on the powers of Charles I and the crown. But this faction was increasingly outnumbered and outmanoeuvred in both Houses by the so-called Presbyterians, who favoured a narrower religious settlement based upon the restoration of a single state church to which everyone must conform and a political and constitutional settlement based upon a deal with the king restoring most of his pre-war powers and largely turning the clock back to autumn 1641. Cromwell intervened several times in debates during autumn and winter 1646, trying to advance the Independent agenda or thwart Presbyterian-backed policies, but generally to little avail. With a numerical advantage in both Houses, the Presbyterians usually dominated parliamentary developments, but they were well aware that a further, potentially far more serious obstacle to their plans lurked outside. With the war won, the parliamentary armies, particularly the New Model Army, had time on their hands. Although the soldiers were themselves divided, the majority favoured the religious and probably the political goals of the Independents and were dismayed by the Presbyterian agenda, which threatened to destroy religious liberty. Thus for the time being parliamentary negotiations with the king were given a low priority. Instead, to clear away the main obstacle to the sort of settlement they wished to pursue and as an essential pre-condition to it, during late 1646 and early 1647 the Presbyterians focused on sidelining, reducing and neutering the parliamentary armies.

During the latter half of 1646 and on through the early months of 1647 Cromwell repeatedly tried to defend the parliamentary armies from attacks upon them inside and outside parliament. For example, in mid-July 1646 he spoke in the Commons in defence of Fairfax and the New Model Army and during the winter he strongly criticised Presbyterian-backed plans swiftly to disband most of the parliamentary forces and compel most of the remaining troops to serve in Ireland, in a long-delayed campaign to reverse the 1641 Irish Catholic rebellion and restore English rule. However, the tide was running against him and his letters to Fairfax reflected a sense of gloom and despondency. Thus in August 1646 he wrote 'We are full of faction and worse', while by March 1647 he was noting that 'there want not in all places men who have so much malice against the army as besots them ... Never were the spirits of men more embittered than now. Surely the Devil hath but a short time'. Cromwell did not entirely despair and retained his belief that God would intervene to make things well and 'overcome all this' – 'But this is our comfort, God is in heaven, and He doth what pleaseth Him; His and only His counsel shall stand, whatever the designs of men, and the fury of the people be', he told Fairfax. But there was little sign of divine intervention in the New Year. Instead Cromwell fell seriously ill with an 'impostume of the head' during January, which laid him low for several weeks, and although better by early March he seems to have attended parliament only infrequently during spring. This may be the first sign of what became one of

'But this is our comfort, God is in heaven, and He doth what pleaseth Him; His and only His counsel shall stand, whatever the designs of men, and the fury of the people be'

Cromwell's traits, physically to withdraw from the theatre of debate if he found the subject distasteful or was clearly losing the argument. And by spring 1647 there was little doubt that Cromwell and his allies were losing the parliamentary arguments, for the dominant Presbyterians swept on to vote through mass disbandment and enforced service in Ireland.

Cromwell returned to the fray in May 1647, one of four officer MPs dispatched by parliament to the headquarters of the New Model Army in Saffron Walden to test the mood of the army. Cromwell and his colleagues became aware of the depth of the soldiers' dismay, their unease at mass disbanding or compulsory service in Ireland and their demands that arrears of military pay be met in full, provision be made for maimed ex-soldiers, military widows and orphans and indemnity be guaranteed against future criminal prosecution for war-time actions. Both during his three weeks in Saffron Walden and before and after when he spoke in the Commons, Cromwell sought to avoid a breakdown in relations between parliament and its armies and urged mutual restraint. Thus he reassured the Commons that the soldiers would obey parliament's orders, though the report he presented after Saffron Walden also highlighted military grievances and requests; he warned that a minority of soldiers might resist enforced disbandment and he advised parliament to make service in Ireland voluntary, not compulsory. Similarly, at Saffron Walden he and his colleagues reassured the regiments that parliament was aware of and responding to their legitimate requests, pointing to recent indemnity legislation and more generous payment of arrears, and he warned the troops to respect and obey parliament's authority.

In reality, relations between the Presbyterian-dominated parliament and the New Model Army were on the brink of collapse. When the parliamentary majority pressed ahead with plans for a swift mass disbandment, the New Model

Sr   your letters about your n
quarters, directed to the houses, c
seasonable, and were to very
purpose, there want not in
places men, whod hand soo n
    against the Armie
inclined as besotts them, the
petition wch suggested a dangr
designd upon the parlmt in co
ingo to those quarters doth su
cient euidence the same, but
gott nothinge by itt, for the ho
did assoyle the Armie from a
suspicion, and hand left you
quarter where you pleasd.
Neuer were the spirits of m
moue inbittered then now, su
the Deuil hath but a shor
tymd, Sr its good the hea
ber fixed against all this,
naked Symplicityd of Christ, u
that wisdom Hee pleasd to gi
and patiencd will ouercom
this, that God would keepe yo
heart as Hee has donn hithe

[left margin, written vertically]

I desire my most humble seruice
may bee presented to my Lady.
Mr Alleu desires col. Barch
gouernor of Readinge may bee remembered
if our expectationd may not bee ni
any frend, there is a desiringe u an
seruice to you.

is the prayer of
your excellencyes most humbl
your seruant

Oliuer Cromwell

During May 1647, New Model Army representatives conferred with a quartet of officer MPs, including Cromwell, at the Sun Inn, Saffron Walden. The late medieval timber-framed building was enlarged during the Tudor and Stuart periods and now has an ornately pargeted facade.
Dr Peter Gaunt

Army took a stand. In late May its council of war refused to obey parliamentary orders and set itself up in direct opposition to parliament, organising mass meetings and setting out its goals. At the same time, a junior officer, Cornet Joyce, and a body of New Model cavalry seized the king, held by parliament in Northamptonshire, and carried him prisoner to Newmarket, where the New Model Army was based. Although Cromwell denied that he had planned or organised any of these developments, and was probably dismayed by them, it is likely that, once parliament voted on 25 May to proceed with disbandment, he foresaw the looming breakdown, and Joyce probably called on Cromwell in London in late May before his expedition. During the last week of May Cromwell sought and obtained from parliament nearly £2000 in the arrears of his own military salary, perhaps because he expected his military career to end in the looming disbandment, but more plausibly to settle his finances before relations collapsed. Recognising that a parting of the ways had been reached – temporarily, he hoped – and that his recent attempts to build bridges between parliament and army had failed, Cromwell decided to throw in his lot with the

New Model Army as it resisted parliament's plans. Sometime on 3 June he left London and joined the army around Newmarket.

For the next six months or more Cromwell was primarily a military-based politician, travelling with the New Model Army and staying in or near its peripatetic headquarters. During the summer Cromwell was with Fairfax and the army as they moved closer to London, to exert pressure on parliament, though they swung westwards and established a base around Reading during July. There, the officers and regimental representatives debated what to do next. Cromwell, who played a prominent role, showed some sympathy for regimental demands for radical reform but he argued strongly and passionately against suggestions that the army march on London to further its programme by purging or expelling parliament. Although he supported moves to persuade parliament itself to suspend or impeach a small group of prominent Presbyterian MPs who had orchestrated moves against the army, he was adamant that the use of naked force against the constitutional authority would irreparably taint anything the army might then impose – 'that [which] you have by force I look upon it as nothing'. Instead, he argued that the New Model Army should proceed to draw up its own religious and constitutional settlement or 'treaty' and then persuade the other parties, especially king and parliament, to accept it. Eventually Cromwell and his colleagues won the argument at Reading and work resumed on the army's document. However, when ten days later a pro-Presbyterian London mob stormed the Palace of Westminster, threatening and frightening off Independent-minded MPs, who swiftly sought the army's protection, Fairfax and Cromwell had no hesitation in leading the New Model Army into London to restore order. This was achieved without serious opposition or bloodshed in early August, and after a show of force most of the army pulled back to bases in and around

Putney, leaving a somewhat overawed but orderly parliament to continue its deliberations. In the wake of this, the Presbyterian clique was chastened and shied away from renewed attacks upon the soldiers, while Independent MPs and peers and other Members sympathetic to the army's agenda spoke with more assurance and influence.

During late summer and early autumn the New Model officers worked on their draft settlement, called the Heads of the Proposals. There is no evidence that Cromwell was closely involved in its preparation and instead his son-in-law, Henry Ireton, probably took the lead, in consultation with other senior officers and pro-army MPs and peers. But to the extent that Cromwell endorsed the document and supported it when he resumed regularly attending the Commons in the autumn, it gives an insight into Cromwell's thinking at this stage. In religion, it envisaged the continuation of something like the old episcopal Church of England, but no one had to adhere to it and instead there was to be broad toleration for other Protestant groups. Politically and constitutionally, the document was cautious and conciliatory, calling for the restoration or continuation of much of the traditional system, with government by crown, Lords and Commons, though parliament was to gain temporary control over the military and executive arms of government, powers which traditionally had rested with the crown alone, and there was provision for a succession of biennial parliaments.

Although king and parliament remained undecided about the Heads of the Proposals and were far from committed to it, the cautious nature of the officers' scheme began to foment unrest in several New Model regiments during autumn 1647. Amongst both common soldiers and junior officers, there was a feeling that senior officers were not going far enough, were too accommodating towards the king and the constitutional status quo and were squandering an opportunity for more extensive reform. In questioning their senior officers and agitating for their own more radical agenda, the New Model regiments were influenced both by their own war-time experiences and beliefs and by the propaganda of several radical pressure groups, particularly the Levellers – the most influential radical group of the later 1640s, who put forward a wide-ranging programme of political, constitutional, social, economic, judicial and religious reforms and who for a time seemed to attract strong military and civilian support, especially in London. By late October, many New Model regiments were supporting an alternative plan, the Agreement of the People, which picked up several Leveller themes. It stressed that sovereignty rested with the people, who held certain inalienable rights, and with their directly elected representatives in the House of Commons. It envisaged a far more powerful Commons elected on a reformed franchise and with redistributed seats and suggested that though both monarchy and House of Lords might survive, they were to be mere figureheads, starved of real power. Attempting to heal growing divisions and produce from these two very different sets of ideas a single draft settlement which the entire army could support, the senior officers convened a series of meetings, held in and around Putney church between 28 October and 11 November, attended by senior officers, regimental representatives and a few other soldiers and civilians. Cromwell chaired the early sessions, and surviving records show in detail the line which he and others took during the opening days of the Putney debates, though we possess only sketchy outlines of the later debates.

Cromwell's broad support for traditional constitutional and social structures, his fear of chaos or social overturning, his emphasis on tight military discipline and his condemnation of anything smacking of insubordination or mutiny all

Cromwell's son-in-law and fellow officer, Henry Ireton, was probably the leading figure in army politics in the later 1640s and his death in Ireland in 1651 was a blow to Cromwell personally and politically. This portrait, perhaps by Robert Walker, dates from around 1649.
National Portrait Gallery

probably inclined him against the radical, Leveller demands which surfaced at Putney. But, as chairman, Cromwell generally kept aloof from the detailed debates, leaving other senior officers such as Ireton to engage the more radical junior officers and troopers on issues such as the nature and source of sovereignty and the extension of the franchise. Instead, Cromwell repeatedly sought to calm tempers, restrain the more radical and hot-headed representatives and remind them of their common duty to God. Stressing the need for unity, he sought to guide discussion by considering the army's existing commitments and statements, but in this, as in most areas, the record suggests that Cromwell failed to stamp his authority on the debates. Similarly, his attempts to achieve consensus by conceding that further modest reforms might be acceptable probably satisfied neither side. On the other hand, Cromwell was far more effective during the second week of November in working with Fairfax and other senior officers to wind up the generally unsatisfactory debates at Putney and order the representatives back to their regiments for a general rendezvous of the army. However much Cromwell may in theory have preferred the path of negotiation, compromise and consensus, in reality at Putney, as on several other occasions during Cromwell's career, that proved difficult, frustrating and ultimately fruitless. At Putney, as elsewhere, he proved far better suited to resolving a problem by swift, decisive confrontation.

The end of the Putney debates on 11 November coincided with the king's escape from Hampton Court, where he was being held by the army. Charles's flight and demonstrable untrustworthiness, compounded by growing evidence that he was negotiating with the Scots to induce them to restore him to power by force through a renewed war, were in many ways very convenient for the senior officers. Negotiations with the king, which had opened up such dangerous divisions within the army, were now terminated – in January 1648 Cromwell and other officer MPs vigorously supported a successful parliamentary motion to end all contacts with Charles – and instead the senior officers could reunite the army to meet the renewed royalist threat. Cromwell and his colleagues did just that at a series of rendezvous held in mid-November, easily crushing a very minor mutiny, and thereafter they ensured that the sort of divisions which had wracked the army during the autumn had little chance to resurface. The king's escape and flight proved so helpful to the officers that there has been speculation that it was engineered, that Cromwell had frightened the king with invented tales of assassination and encouraged him to run by deliberately withdrawing the guards. However, once more no clear evidence supports the conspiracy theories and it is most unlikely that Cromwell would have welcomed the prospect of Charles at liberty, perhaps in the Channel Isles or on the Continent, organising a renewed war. Moreover, there are reports that Cromwell and Fairfax were both surprised and relieved to learn that Charles had instead merely crossed to the Isle of Wight, where he was intercepted and imprisoned by the local parliamentarian commander.

In the closing weeks of 1647 and on through the opening months of 1648, Cromwell continued to divide his time between parliament and the army head-quarters around Windsor. As the king laid plans for renewed war, concluding a deal with the Scots and encouraging his supporters in England and Wales to rise up, so

'You see how God hath honoured and blessed every resolute action of these for Him; doubt not but He will do so still'

Cromwell's comments about Charles became colder, often twinned with calls for parliament and the army to stand firm and obey God's will. He advised the governor of Carisbrooke castle on the Isle of Wight, the king's new gaoler, to keep the king under close guard – 'You see how God hath honoured and blessed every resolute action of these for Him; doubt not but He will do so still'. In another letter to the governor he referred to the king's flight and subsequent developments as 'a mighty providence to this poor kingdom and to us all' for 'the House of Commons is very sensible of the King's dealings, and of our brethren's', the latter a reference to the Scots. In the Commons he suggested that the army's former support of monarchy was now in doubt because the king had broken 'his trust'.

By spring 1648 the uneasy peace was collapsing with the onset of what is sometimes dubbed the second civil war. Between March and October poorly coordinated risings occurred in many parts of England and Wales, some overtly pro-royalist from the outset, others beginning more ambiguously as anti-parliamentarian rebellions. Most were put down by local garrisons and forces, but some grew more serious and required the intervention of senior commanders and units of the New Model Army. Thus on 30 April Cromwell was ordered west, leading several New Model regiments to put down serious rebellion in South Wales. In fact, before he arrived local troops had defeated the main rebel army outside Cardiff, and Cromwell led what amounted to a large mopping up operation, though a difficult one, retaking Chepstow and Tenby en route to investing the main rebel stronghold, the walled town and castle of Pembroke. The operation against Pembroke proved long and frustrating and tied Cromwell down for several weeks, from 24 May until mid-July. Attempts to storm the town were repulsed, Cromwell had to wait for heavy guns to arrive before he could mount an effective bombardment and not until 11 July did the defenders surrender.

Cromwell was anxious to conclude the operation, because in line with their agreement with the king, the Scots had raised a royalist army of invasion which had crossed the border in early July and began moving south through England, following the west coast route. Pembroke secured, Cromwell moved north to intercept it, but he chose to march via the Midlands to pick up supplies and through Yorkshire to rendezvous with reinforcements before turning west, crossing the Pennines into Lancashire. Cromwell therefore fell in behind the Scottish army, in theory leaving open the road to London, presumably the Scots' ultimate objective, but more importantly blocking their line of retreat to their homeland. On 17 August Cromwell attacked and destroyed a large part of the poorly organised and dangerously strung-out Scottish army outside Preston. Over the following days, in a series of running fights, he pursued and cut down remaining Scottish units, particularly cavalry, in a string of engagements along the road south through Winwick to Warrington. As usual, Cromwell detected 'the great hand of God in this business' – 'Give glory to God for this unspeakable mercy'.

The renewed fighting of 1648 caused a clear hardening in the attitude of the victorious parliamentary forces. Following a prolonged siege at Colchester, Fairfax had two leading royalists executed and Cromwell dispatched to London a trio of rebel leaders whom he captured at Pembroke, all of whom were later condemned though only one was executed. But many in the army believed that principal responsibility for the renewed bloodshed rested with the king and demanded that he face justice. They were aghast when, even as they were fighting the royalists, parliament reopened negotiations with the king on the Isle of Wight, hoping to forestall the army's talk of exemplary justice by swiftly reaching a settlement with Charles and restoring him to power in London. For a time, an

A Case for *Noll Cromwells* Nose; with the cure of *Tom Fairfax* his Gout.

O Yes ! O Yes ! O Yes !

IF any Man, Angell or Devill can tell where the bodies of Oliver Cromwell and Tom Fairfax are now resident, you may know the one by his refulgent copper nose, which he ever kept well burnisht, that so he might not be constrained to trouble the devill to light him, or grope out his way to helle you may know the other by his smoakie countenance, his mouth is drawn awry, and he looks like the picture of Doomsday, when the Planets be darkned ; if any as aforesaid can bring tale or tyding, where the two Archtraytors aforesaid now are, let him bring word to the cryer, and he shall be well rewarded.

God save the King and------the Parliament.

angry and sceptical army watched as parliament's plans moved forward rather unsteadily, but in early December it decided to pounce. The New Model Army entered London virtually unopposed and purged the House of Commons of all MPs deemed to be in favour of a settlement with the king or antagonistic to the army and its agenda; this operation became known as Pride's Purge. That left behind a small 'rump' of a few dozen MPs, hard men who were willing to do the army's bidding and ensure that the king faced justice. Over the next few weeks, working hand in hand with the army and ignoring a much depleted and uncooperative House of Lords, these MPs set up a mechanism to try the king and facilitated his trial and execution in January 1649. They then swept on during the following weeks formally to abolish monarchy and the House of Lords and declare England and Wales a republic. Those in parliament and the army who supported these developments were probably motivated by secular or religious factors. For some, cold reasons of state determined that the king should die, for he had proved himself completely untrustworthy and only too willing to renew civil war and there would be no chance for durable peace and a firm settlement while he lived. For others, their perception of the will of God was probably uppermost in their minds. They believed that, following God's clear support for the cause in the victories of 1645–46, the difficulties of 1647 and renewed war of 1648 demonstrated that they had lost the support of the Lord and had failed to obey Him; after much heart-searching, they decided that their error had been to negotiate with the king in 1647 and attempt to reach a settlement with him, apparently against God's will, and they concluded that God therefore demanded the destruction of Charles I and perhaps monarchy as well.

Historians are deeply divided over the role which Cromwell played in these developments, the timing of his decision to support the trial and execution and the reasons which led him to support that course. We know that Cromwell took his seat in the Commons after the military purge in December, that he supported the mechanism then put in place to try the king and that during January he was an active participant in the trial itself, sitting as one of the judges and signing the death warrant. But much else is unclear and open to historical debate. It is likely that in this area, as in so much during Cromwell's life, his faith and interpretation of God's will guided him. He attended part or all of an intense, three-day prayer meeting of the army officers at Windsor in late April, just before they went off to fight, and probably shared the general conclusion reached on that occasion that, when the opportunity presented itself, they should 'call Charles Stuart, that man of blood, to an account for that blood he had shed'. In the course of the fighting, he became more confident of God's will, writing in late June that the Lord did not wish the nation to be the 'object of wrath and anger', to have 'our necks

This Dutch satirical print of 1649 portrays Cromwell as an arch-hypocrite and a power-hungry usurper, for even as Charles I is being beheaded in Whitehall, Cromwell is seizing the power and emblems of monarchy, including ermine robe, orb, crown and sword of justice.
British Museum

WITHAL

under a yoke of bondage', and that He would break 'the rod of the oppressor'. More starkly, after Preston he advised the Speaker to do God's work, reminding him that 'even Kings' might be reproved by God, and urging him to secure 'the peace and welfare of the people' and to ensure that 'they that are implacable and will not leave troubling the Land may speedily be destroyed out of the land'. In November he told Fairfax that he shared his troops' opinion that there should be 'impartial justice done upon Offenders' and was persuaded that these sentiments 'are things which God puts into our hearts'. Around the same time, in two letters to the governor of Carisbrooke, Cromwell condemned the renewed attempts to do a deal with Charles, against whom God had so clearly 'witnessed', and he argued that an honest, godly party – such as the army, on whom God had lavished His providences – had the right to overthrow any majority party or 'outward authority' opposing God's will, perhaps indicating support for the military purge of parliament which would soon follow. All this might suggest that by autumn 1648 at the latest, and perhaps as early as the spring, Cromwell had concluded that direct military intervention and regicide was the best course because willed by God.

On the other hand, there are signs that Cromwell did not decide to support this course anywhere near as clearly or as early as this. Having defeated the Scots in and south of Preston in mid-August, Cromwell travelled to Scotland to support the new pro-parliamentary regime which had seized power there in the wake of the collapse of the Scottish-royalist faction. He remained in Scotland until mid-October, but then progressed south only as far as Yorkshire, where he spent November in a curiously inactive siege operation against the isolated royalist base of Pontefract castle, writing that he and his colleagues 'were in a waiting posture, desiring to see what the Lord would lead us to'. At length, having been summoned back to London by Fairfax, he did come south, arriving in London on the evening of 6 December, a few hours after the military purge of parliament. His words, movements and timing suggest a man still hesitant and undecided about what the Lord wished, acquiescing rather than actively participating in a coup against parliament. Moreover, some contemporary sources revealed rumours that during mid- and late December Cromwell was still exploring the possibility of a settlement between Charles and the army and a newspaper alleged that at an army meeting on Christmas Day Cromwell remained unconvinced by regicide, declaring 'there was no policy in taking away his life'. If Cromwell was a late and hesitant convert to regicide, his doubts seem to have been subsiding by the beginning of January, for around that time he declared in the Commons that 'since the Providence of God hath cast this upon us, I cannot but submit to Providence, though I am not yet provided to give you my advice'. On another occasion, he declared that he had been guided by 'Providence and necessity', intertwining the will of God with the dictates of unfolding events. By the time the trial itself opened, on 20 January, Cromwell had been won over by his interpretation of God's will and he actively supported the

regicide. In several later letters and speeches he strongly and unambiguously defended the trial and execution, seeing them as the just will of God and justifying them through biblical references, for only 'exemplary justice upon the prime leader of all this quarrel', he argued, would save the nation from God's wrath and secure His continuing favour.

By early 1649 Cromwell had come through a period of fire, had emerged from the midst of trouble, and he began looking towards the 'glorious mercies' which might now flow from God. But the price had been enormous – the fracturing of the parliamentary cause, the failure and abandonment of many of his earlier principles and goals, the acceptance of the army's intervention in government, and with it the destruction of much of the traditional constitution which Cromwell had once held dear. But in the end Cromwell's faith reconciled him to this turn of events, for he came to believe that these developments had been willed by God and that the Lord was guiding him along this unforeseen and unexpected path towards a better place.

'I think there is more cause of danger
from disunion amongst ourselves
than by anything from our enemies'

Power-broker 1649–53

*'Truly notwithstanding you have brought this work to this issue, yet it seems your work
is not at an end. You have yet another enemy to encounter with, and friends to stand by.
The interest you have fought for you have yet further to make good'*
(from Cromwell's speech to the General Council of the army, March 1649)

In spring 1649 Cromwell addressed his army colleagues, reviewing what
parliament and the army had achieved thus far but also setting out what still
lay ahead. He warned his audience that they had to defeat enemies at home
and abroad, but that far greater dangers lay in potential divisions within the
parliamentary cause itself – 'as a poor man that desires to see the work of God
to prosper in our hands, I think there is more cause of danger from disunion
amongst ourselves than by anything from our enemies'. If they remained united
in pursuit of God's cause and the execution of His will, 'doing our duty and
waiting upon the Lord, we shall find He will be as a wall of brass round about
us till we have finished that work that He has for us to do'. But great dangers
lurked should they 'depart from God and disunite by that departure and fall into
disunion amongst ourselves'. Cromwell's speech proved remarkably prescient and
set out his agenda for the following five years, down to the end of 1653. It was a
period which, for Cromwell, fell into two halves, both in different ways reflecting
his enhanced position as a power-broker for the new English regime. Down to
autumn 1651 he was an active military commander, almost permanently on
campaign, helping first to restore discipline within the parliamentary army in
England and then leading a large part of that army on campaigns in Ireland and
Scotland which broke resistance to the new republican regime and paved the way
for full English control. But from autumn 1651, as a full-time, London-based
politician, Cromwell became immersed in the complexities of running the new

THE
Right Honorable
and vndaunted Warrior
OLIVER CROMWELL
Lo: Governour of
IRELAND

state, struggling to persuade politicians to work in harmony with the army to fulfil God's will and becoming all too aware of renewed discords within the parliamentary cause. Although he sought to hold the centrifugal forces in check and restore godly unity, eventually his interpretation of God's will led him to use military might to bring down the constitutional authority and experiment with new forms which he hoped would do the Lord's work.

During 1649–53 Cromwell found himself pulled in different directions. Most obviously, he was a very senior military figure, tied to the army as his power-base and, he believed, an instrument of God's will. But he was also now a very substantial politician and influential parliamentarian with ideas about the religious and political course which the republic should follow, and which he could express from autumn 1651 as he reimmersed himself in parliamentary and civilian politics. But overlying and sharpening this military–civilian dichotomy, Cromwell was torn between two objectives which might crudely be labelled 'conservative' and 'radical'. Cromwell supported the existing social hierarchy and much of the traditional governmental system, and was apprehensive of disorder, indiscipline or anarchy. After 1649 this side of Cromwell favoured 'healing and settling', as he called it, conserving and restoring much of the established political system, returning to traditional civilian forms, perhaps reconciling the nation to the changes which had occurred and rekindling old friendships and alliances. But part of Cromwell, dissatisfied with the imperfect, sinful status quo, felt impelled by God to advocate and advance a rolling programme of radical reform involving the pursuit of religious and civil liberties, especially liberty of conscience for Protestants, and a package of personal, social and judicial reforms, often termed 'godly reformation' or the 'reformation of manners', to moderate the harshest elements of the social and legal systems, allow fewer opportunities for sin and

encourage godliness. In some ways these objectives appeared incompatible. Thus it was unlikely that any freely elected, freely operating traditional parliament would commit itself to radical, godly reform. Equally, the continuing presence of a large and expensive army, Cromwell's ultimate power-base and his reservoir of godliness, impeded moves towards a traditional, low-tax, low-spend, civilian political system. The conservative and radical goals might also create personal tensions and pull Cromwell in different directions at different times.

During winter 1648–49 Cromwell had been pushed towards the radical agenda, acquiescing in the military intervention in government and supporting regicide. Perhaps in reaction to this, during the first half of 1649 Cromwell comes across as more cautious. He regularly sat in the purged remnant or 'Rump' of the House of Commons, from where he unsuccessfully opposed the abolition of the House of Lords as needlessly provocative. Cromwell was one of those sitting MPs who courted Members who, although not purged by the army, had chosen to absent themselves while the king was being tried and executed, and with some success he sought to persuade some to retake their seats and give greater strength and legitimacy to the Rump. Wearing his military hat, during spring 1649 Cromwell acted decisively to help crush an army mutiny in southern England, accompanying Fairfax and loyal regiments as they swooped on the mutineers' base of Burford, Oxfordshire, in mid-May and crushing the mutiny in a largely bloodless show of force, though three ringleaders were swiftly tried and executed.

By May 1649 Cromwell's thoughts were turning to Ireland, for earlier in the year he had accepted command of a military expedition there to restore English rule and crush Catholic and royalist opposition. Still second-in-command of the army under Fairfax, who was to remain in England, an initially hesitant Cromwell had agreed in late March to lead a force comprising 12,000 New Model troops,

judging Ireland the greatest and most urgent threat to the English regime, bitterly
condemning the 'barbarism' of the Irish rebels – later in 1649 he referred to the
Irish as 'barbarous and bloodthirsty' – and seeing the campaign as furthering
God's work. Before embarking, he spent several months based first in London and
then, from late July, in south Pembrokeshire, ensuring that the expedition would
be well supplied. Sailing from Milford Haven around 14 August, it landed
unopposed near Dublin the following day.

Cromwell's Irish expedition, the only occasion on which he campaigned or
travelled outside the British mainland, lasted a little over nine months, from mid-
August 1649 until late May 1650. Marked by sieges not battles, the campaign was
also geographically limited, for Cromwell focused on restoring English control

Opposite: Cahir castle, beside the river Suir, was one of the largest medieval fortresses in Ireland. However, when Cromwell brought up heavy guns and warned the garrison 'if I be necessitated to bend my cannon upon you, you must expect what is usual in such cases', the governor soon surrendered.
Dr Peter Gaunt

over Leinster and Munster, securing strongpoints along or close to the eastern and southern coasts, never straying more than forty miles inland. From Dublin he struck north, to secure the main coast road and strongholds along it; having taken Drogheda in mid-September Cromwell returned south, leaving other commanders to lead detached units into Ulster. Instead, Cromwell next secured the coast road south from Dublin, including the capture of Wexford. During the winter and spring he besieged a string of strongholds in southern Ireland, campaigning as far north as Cashel and Kilkenny, as far west as Cork and Mallow. At length, responding to urgent calls for him to return to the mainland, on 26 May 1650 he sailed from Youghal and landed near Bristol.

In many ways Cromwell's Irish campaign was a great success. Although he campaigned in only parts of the island and it was left to commanders who succeeded him to mop up and capture rebel towns such as Limerick and Galway, Cromwell broke the back of Irish resistance and effectively restored English rule to much of Ireland. Several rebel strongholds fell to him by force, notably Drogheda, Wexford, Kilkenny and Clonmel, while others, such as New Ross, Fethard, Cashel and Cahir, promptly surrendered with little or no opposition, and diplomacy led to a handful of bases opening their gates to the English, including Cork, Youghal, Kinsale and Bandon. On the other hand, there were also problems and failures. Cromwell's army succumbed to disease during the Irish winter – he described 2 December as the most 'terrible a day as ever I marched in, in all my life' – and he had lain 'very sick' and 'crazy in my health' for a fortnight or so in late October and early November. A mixture of Irish resistance, their strong defences and the disruption to the English campaign through illness and bad weather caused several operations to become bogged down or fail. Cromwell had to abandon the sieges of Duncannon and Waterford and although both Kilkenny

and Clonmel eventually surrendered, they resisted stoutly and repulsed
Cromwell's attempts to take them by storm. On both occasions this had led
to substantial English losses, especially the disastrous and ill-conceived attack
on Clonmel on 16 May, which left between 1000 and 2500 parliamentary troops
dead and was by some way both the New Model Army's blackest day and
Cromwell's costliest operation.

However, historical assessments of Cromwell in Ireland usually focus
on what occurred when Drogheda and Wexford fell to his army in September
and October 1649 respectively. Although the two events are usually bracketed
together, the circumstances were different. At Drogheda, once the defenders had
rejected a summons to surrender and the English army successfully stormed the
town, Cromwell made a conscious decision to deny quarter and put to the sword
not only the garrison but also male townspeople found actively supporting and
assisting the garrison and any Catholic friars discovered in the town. Most of
the garrison of 3100 and several hundred townsmen perished. At Wexford the
defenders also rejected an initial summons and Cromwell's guns opened up
the wall. But at this point, Cromwell offered to accept an orderly surrender and
guarantee the lives of garrison and townspeople. However, while negotiations were
underway, the commander of Wexford castle surrendered and admitted English
troops, who took the opportunity to enter the town. When some of the garrison,
supported by townsmen, resisted, the English army brutally crushed opposition;
before order was restored, around 2000 defenders perished. While at Drogheda
Cromwell had deliberately pursued a policy of denying quarter, the bloodletting
at Wexford seems to have been unplanned and unexpected, though surviving
sources suggest that Cromwell neither deplored nor made much effort to halt it.

According to contemporary rules of war, defenders of a stronghold who,

> 'I am persuaded that this is a righteous judgment of God upon these barbarous wretches, who have imbrued their hands in so much innocent blood'

surrounded and summoned to surrender, refused, might expect no mercy if it subsequently fell by force. This practice, seen only rarely during the civil wars in England and Wales but more often in internal Scottish conflicts of the mid-1640s and on the Continent, was designed to save lives overall, for it would encourage other strongholds to surrender swiftly and so without bloodshed on either side. Indeed, in his letters after Drogheda Cromwell commented that 'I believe this bitterness will save much effusion of blood, through the goodness of God' and that the brutality there 'will tend to prevent the effusion of blood for the future, which are satisfactory grounds to such actions, which otherwise cannot but work remorse and regret'. Moreover, at neither town was the slaughter indiscriminate. Unarmed male civilians who were not actively defending the town and supporting the garrison generally survived, and there is only one reference to women or children perishing, when at Wexford several overloaded boats carrying townspeople accidentally capsized and around 300 drowned. But Drogheda and Wexford trouble historians and are often seen as blots on Cromwell's career. Cromwell was a man of his times, locked into the cycle of violence between Irish and English. He had been greatly affected by the massacre of several thousand Protestants in Ireland during 1641–42 at the hands of the Irish Catholic rebels. In strident language which jars to a modern ear, he justified the deaths at Drogheda and Wexford as just and godly vengeance for that massacre. 'I am persuaded that this is a righteous judgment of God upon these barbarous wretches, who have imbrued their hands in so much innocent blood', he wrote after Drogheda, and he described the deaths at Wexford as God's 'righteous justice,…a just judgment upon them,…who in their piracies had made preys of so many families, and made with their bloods to answer the cruelties which they had exercised upon the lives of divers poor Protestants'. In fact, many who

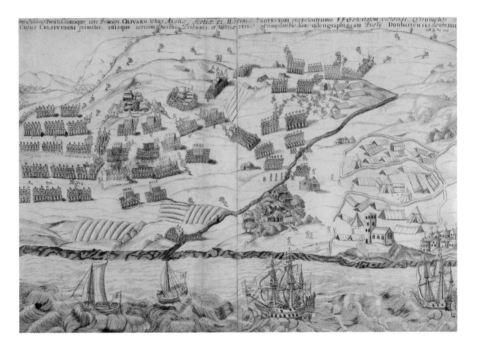

perished were not Irish Catholics or had played little part in the 1641 rising.

Cromwell returned to England in spring 1650 to help meet the threat from Scotland. The Scots had declared Charles I's eldest son king of Britain and were gathering an army to restore him to power in England and enforce Presbyterianism. Fairfax was reluctant to lead an expedition into Scotland, and although Cromwell and others sought to dissuade him – very half-heartedly, some critics claimed, though the evidence is inconclusive – Fairfax resigned. Cromwell, long second-in-command and now conqueror of Ireland, was the only plausible successor and on 28 June the Rump appointed him Lord General and commander-in-chief. On that day Cromwell left London to lead 16,000 New Model troops north, to campaign in Scotland rather than await a likely invasion. The campaign lasted just over a year, from late July 1650, when he left Berwick, until August 1651, when he recrossed the Tweed.

Although punctuated by magnificent victories, Cromwell's Scottish campaign was often static, and he was wary of a canny foe who used the defences and topography of Scotland to great effect. Thus instead of defending the border, the Scottish army pulled back into the strongly defended area around Edinburgh and Leith, allowing Cromwell free access to the southern lowlands but refusing to offer battle in the open, even when the English approached Edinburgh several times during August; for his part, Cromwell felt unable to attack the Scots' position. By early September fruitless marches, bad weather, over-stretched supply lines and attempts to live off a land denuded by the Scots were taking their toll, and disease was rife in the English army. Cromwell trudged back to Dunbar to regroup. Seeing their opportunity, the Scots pounced, moving south quickly to occupy the hill overlooking Dunbar and blocking the road south. The Scottish army significantly outnumbered the fit troops available to Cromwell, perhaps by nearly two to one, and the letter which Cromwell wrote to the governor of Newcastle on the evening of 2 September betrayed his feelings – Cromwell was edgy, acknowledged his 'very difficult' position, recognised the possibility of defeat but placed his fate in the hands of 'the only wise God...of whose mercy we have had large experience'. Rather than waiting to be picked off, Cromwell decided to attack and a little before dawn on 3 September he engaged the Scots, who seem to have been taken by surprise. Moreover, as at Preston, Cromwell ensured that his men never engaged the full strength of the opposing army. He initially attacked and broke the eastern, coastal end of the Scottish line, before tearing into the centre of the now shaken and disorganised Scottish army. As the sun rose and the Scots broke, Cromwell cried 'Now let God arise and His enemies shall be scattered'. According to one account, Cromwell halted his front line to sing together Psalm 117 before pursuing the Scots. The casualty figures which Cromwell claimed, of 3000 Scottish dead and 10,000 prisoners against 30 parliamentary dead, seem remarkable and many more Scots may have got away to fight another day. Yet Dunbar was a stunning victory, triggering in Cromwell an even more acute awareness of God's support – 'This is the Lord's doing and it is marvellous in our eyes', 'The Lord hath showed us an exceeding mercy: who can tell how great it is', 'one of the most signal mercies God hath done for England and His people, this war'.

Stunning as it was, Dunbar altered the location but not the shape of the stand-off between English and Scots. In the aftermath of battle, Cromwell rolled up the rest of the lowlands without serious resistance, securing Edinburgh and Glasgow. Meanwhile, the Scots fell back into the highlands, made Stirling their new base, and quickly regrouped and rebuilt their army. Once more the result was stalemate. Cromwell approached Stirling several times but felt unable to attack it and he could not tempt out the Scots to give battle. A propaganda campaign for the hearts and minds of the people, weaning them from royalism with talk of common cause, faith and goals, generally fell as flat as attempts to show that the Scots were disobeying God in taking up arms against His chosen people, the English. The Scottish winter put paid to active campaigning for several weeks and in early February Cromwell fell seriously ill and spent the next few months sick or convalescing in Edinburgh, unable to retake the field until mid-summer 1651.

Fit again, Cromwell determined to break the logjam and avoid a second winter in Scotland, 'to the ruin' of his army. In late July he threw much of his army across the Forth, threatening Stirling from the east and north-east and occupying the agricultural land of Fife, upon which the Scottish forces depended. Meanwhile, he left the lowlands thinly guarded, tempting the Scots southwards to attempt an invasion of England. Cromwell's calm, confident response when the Scots did just this in early August suggests that he anticipated, even welcomed, it. He organised English troops to shadow the Scottish-royalist army as it followed the west coast route, while he moved south. Having picked up very little support en route, by late August the Scottish-royalist army was holed up in Worcester. Cromwell joined English forces massing there and by the beginning of September he had over 30,000 men, hugely outnumbering the Scots. Cromwell waited until 3 September, the anniversary of Dunbar, to give battle. The Scots fought fiercely but were defeated utterly, and while Charles Stuart, styling himself Charles II, narrowly escaped, Worcester destroyed Scottish royalism as an effective force. Though victory was hardly surprising, as usual Cromwell saw Worcester as a gift from God – 'The dimensions of this mercy are above my thoughts. It is, for aught I know, a crowning mercy'. It was the last time Cromwell led his troops into battle, although he remained commander-in-chief until his death. In autumn 1651 he returned to London, the conquering hero, retook his seat in the Rump and resumed his political career, joining his family in lodgings off Whitehall.

The story of Cromwell's relations with the Rump parliament – the purged remnant of the House of Commons of the Long Parliament that governed England and Wales from December 1648 onwards – in the eighteen months after Worcester is disappointingly thin, for the surviving sources are meagre. Cromwell seems to have been playing his cards close to his chest and there are few surviving letters from this period. Cromwell attended the Rump and its Council of State

'curb the proud and the insolent;...
relieve the oppressed, hear the
groans of poor prisoners in England;
be pleased to reform the abuses of all
professions; and if there be any one
that makes many poor to make a few
rich, that suits not a Commonwealth'

quite regularly, though he absented himself from both for a time in spring 1653.
But down to April 1653, we have no full and reliable record of any parliamentary
speech delivered by Cromwell. With so little evidence available, much weight is
often given to records of two conversations which Cromwell had at this time
with the politician and diplomat Bulstrode Whitelocke. On both occasions
Cromwell was exploring options for constitutional change and expressed
qualified support for 'a settlement with somewhat of the Monarchical power in
it'. At the second meeting, in November 1652, Cromwell reportedly went further,
bitterly condemning the Rump as full of 'pride, and ambition, and self-seeking',
hopelessly divided into factions, unable and unwilling to institute godly reforms.
The MPs, Cromwell felt, 'will destroy again what the Lord hath done graciously
for them and us'.

However, in reconstructing Cromwell's relations with the Rump between
autumn 1651 and spring 1653, historians generally rely heavily upon Cromwell's
earlier letters and utterances while on campaign and upon speeches he made
after the Rump had ended. In Ireland and Scotland Cromwell had become even
more aware of God's support and the need to repay the Lord by pursuing godly
reforms. In particular, the victories secured over the Scottish royalists had brought
out the radical Cromwell, impressed upon him the urgency of God's message
and led him to urge godly reform on the Rump. After Dunbar he called on
parliament to 'curb the proud and the insolent;...relieve the oppressed, hear
the groans of poor prisoners in England; be pleased to reform the abuses of all
professions; and if there be any one that makes many poor to make a few rich,
that suits not a Commonwealth'. After a victory at Inverkeithing in July 1651,
when his troops cleared the north bank of the Forth, Cromwell advised the
Rump to ensure that 'the common weal may more and more be sought, and

Opposite: This contemporary though somewhat imaginative Dutch print of the ejection of the Rump shows Cromwell dismissing the MPs, while in the background other officers and musketeers clear the chamber, encourage the Speaker to vacate the chair and seize documents from the clerks' table.
British Museum

justice done impartially'. After Worcester, Cromwell again urged the Rump 'to do the will of Him who hath done His will for it, and for the nation;…and that justice and righteousness, mercy and truth may flow from you, as a thankful return to our gracious God'. But for several reasons, including the caution and conservatism of the majority of MPs, their suspicion of the army's agenda, and sheer overwork, the Rump moved much more slowly than Cromwell and his colleagues hoped and their reformist aspirations remained unfulfilled. Little was done to achieve liberty of conscience, advance godly reformation or address social and judicial problems.

Cromwell later recalled that after Worcester he had returned to the Commons confident that 'the mercies that God had shewed, the expectations that were in the hearts of all good men, would have prompted those in authority to have done those good things, which might by honest men have been judged a return fit for such a God and worthy of such mercies'. However, that confidence had been shattered by the Rump's failure to respond to his and God's calls to action, even in the wake of army petitions and meetings which Cromwell held with leading MPs – 'I was much disappointed of my expectation', he later recalled. By late 1652 Cromwell was muttering that 'we all forget God, and God will forget us, and give us up to confusion; and these men [the MPs] will help it on, if they be suffered to proceed in their ways; some course must be thought on to curb and restrain them, or we shall be ruined by them'. After effectively withdrawing for a time from the Rump and its Council, probably to clarify his ideas and seek the Lord, on 20 April 1653 Cromwell dramatically intervened to curb and restrain the Rump. Speaking in the House, he angrily condemned the Rump for its 'injustice, delays of justice, self-interest and other faults' and then called in troops to eject the MPs and permanently close the parliament.

Although Cromwell's ejection of the Rump rested upon his long and growing disillusionment with it, his actions on 20 April were triggered by something more specific. In spring 1653 the Rump debated a bill to settle the constitution, and in part Cromwell acted to kill it off, either because it contained something which he considered dangerous, against God's will, or because he mistakenly believed it included such provision. Meeting with leading MPs during the third week of April, Cromwell believed he had won agreement that the bill would not proceed in its present form, so when he heard on 20 April that the House was debating it, he was furious and destroyed the Rump. Exactly what the bill contained which so angered Cromwell and the army remains unclear. The bill itself has not survived and Cromwell's later explanations of its provisions and his response were vague and inconsistent. It may be that Cromwell acted because he believed – rightly or wrongly – that the bill allowed existing Rump MPs to retain their seats almost indefinitely, without facing fresh elections, and that it would merely fill seats vacant after the 1648 purge. Such a scheme, perpetuating the Rump as the core of a half-new parliament, was unacceptable to Cromwell and the army. Alternatively, Cromwell later suggested that the bill provided for an unbroken succession of parliaments, each succeeding the old without a break, so ensuring that full legislative and executive powers would always rest with parliament alone. Cromwell later condemned such an arrangement and supported a system in which parliaments sat from time to time and exercised legislative power, while a completely separate body held executive power and ran government during the substantial intervals between parliaments. A third explanation, which Cromwell stressed in a speech of July 1653, just a few weeks later, claimed that the bill would have provided for the dissolution of the Rump and fresh elections for a completely new parliament – something which Cromwell and the army had been strongly urging for some time – but that the elections would have been too free and open, with no qualifications on those entitled to vote and no control over who could stand and serve as MPs. Rather tardily, Cromwell and his army colleagues came to realise that completely free elections would return royalists, Presbyterians and others, producing a parliament even more hostile to the army than the Rump and less inclined to pursue godly reformation and liberty of conscience.

Having ended England's only legitimate parliamentary government, Cromwell was now the only clear, effective authority left at the centre. He later suggested that all power had passed to him, something which made him uneasy, claiming in later speeches that he was troubled at holding such power and fearful it might corrupt him, and asserting that from the outset he had been keen 'to be quit of the power God had most providentially put into my hand'. Indeed, his actions suggest that he shied away from the 'boundless' authority which had passed to him in April and wished to be divested of it, giving the lie to allegations that Cromwell was motivated by the pursuit of personal power and unlimited political authority. He also stressed that the army had not acted 'to grasp after the 'if the poorest Christian, the most mistaken Christian, should desire to live peaceably and quietly under you,...let him be protected'

power ourselves, to keep it in a military hand, no not for a day'. Cromwell and his colleagues soon reinstated semi-civilian rule, by the end of April establishing an interim Council of State. Designed to keep government ticking over until something more durable was in place, it comprised a mixture of senior officers, including Cromwell, and prominent civilian politicians. Meanwhile, the future settlement of the country was debated by the Council of Officers, 30–40 senior officers chaired by Cromwell. In May, the officers decided to establish a new supreme legislative and executive assembly, made up of around 140 members, on paper representing England, Wales, Scotland and Ireland, though nominated by the Council of Officers rather than elected by the people, selected on the grounds of their godliness and the expectation that they would advance godly reforms. Cromwell claimed to have nominated very few members himself, though the writs appointing them went out in his name. The officers envisaged this Nominated Assembly, also referred to as the Little Parliament, the Parliament of Saints or the Barebones Parliament, as a medium-term solution, holding power for around eighteen months, handing over to a second nominated assembly for a further year and then, in the mid-1650s, making way for elections and a return to more traditional parliaments.

Cromwell did not sit in the Nominated Assembly, which was almost exclusively civilian, and he declined an invitation to join the Council it appointed. He did, however, open the Assembly on 4 July with a major speech, exultant in tone, redolent with religious enthusiasm, full of religious language and references to God's providences. The Assembly, he said, had been 'called by God to rule with Him and for Him', and he urged it to pursue godly reforms, propagate the gospel and secure liberty of conscience – 'have a care of the whole flock. Love all the sheep, love the lambs, love all, and tender all, and cherish all,

Opposite: The only known
contemporary image of the Nominated
Assembly summoned by Cromwell shows
it assembled and organised like a
traditional House of Commons. Its
accuracy is questionable, for it portrays
many more than the 140 or so members
who actually sat in the Assembly. From
The True Manner of the Sitting of the
Parliament of the Commonwealth of
England, 1653.
The British Library, 669, f.17 (39)

and countenance all in all things that are good. And if the poorest Christian,
the most mistaken Christian, should desire to live peaceably and quietly under
you,…let him be protected'. Cromwell closed by stressing that he was resigning
political power to it as 'the supreme authority'. In practice, Cromwell intervened
little in political affairs over the coming months and the Assembly was left to
govern undisturbed. It is remarkable how quickly Cromwell faded into the
background from July, though he continued to conduct routine military business
as Lord General. Perhaps it would have been better if Cromwell had played a
stronger role, guiding the Assembly, for it soon became deeply divided between
moderate reformers and far more radical members who sought to sweep away
existing religious and judicial frameworks, even though nothing had been agreed
and established to put in their place. By late August Cromwell was worried by
this turn of events, writing gloomily that 'the saints' were of such 'different
judgments, and of each sort most seeking to propagate their own, that spirit
of kindness that is to them all, is hardly accepted of any'. But still he did not
intervene. By late 1653 the moderate majority, sharing Cromwell's pessimism, had
had enough and, in a clearly planned move, on 12 December they signed a letter
resigning their powers back to Cromwell. He claimed to have been surprised by
the resignation and to have played no part in planning it – 'I did not know one
tittle of that resignation, until they all came and brought it'. In hindsight,
Cromwell came to speak ruefully of the Assembly as 'a disappointment to our
hopes' and 'a story of my own weakness and folly', noting that 'the issue was not
answerable to the simplicity and honesty of the design' and that 'it hath much
teaching in it, and I hope will make us all wiser for the future'.

In mid-December 1653, for the second time in eight months, the
constitutional system had collapsed, Cromwell was the principal if not the only

power-broker in the nation and all authority in government effectively reverted
to him. In many ways, therefore, the period 1649–53 had ended in failure, for the
nation as for Cromwell, because whatever the triumphs in Ireland and Scotland,
at home the country had been plunged back into constitutional uncertainty and
neither of Cromwell's own agenda – healing and settling and godly reformation –
had made much progress. Indeed, in destroying the last vestige of the duly elected
Long Parliament in spring 1653 Cromwell appeared to have broken with
constitutional legitimacy and set back both settlement and reform, and many
erstwhile colleagues in the parliamentary cause were dismayed, angered or
alienated by his actions; his failed experiment with a novel, non-elected assembly
did little to reconcile or reassure them. While Cromwell's main military objectives
had largely been achieved by this stage, his political and religious goals remained
elusive. In December 1653, as in spring 1649, Cromwell's work was far from at
an end.

Head of state 1653–58

'I look on this to be the great duty of my place, as being set on a watch-tower, to see what may be for the good of these nations and what may be for the preventing of evil,…that good may be attained and that evil…may be obviated'
(from Cromwell's speech to his second Protectorate Parliament, January 1658)

On 16 December 1653 Cromwell became head of state of a united Britain as Lord Protector, accepting a position which years later he likened to that of a watchman, promoting good and warding off evil; he also compared his position to that of 'a good constable to keep the peace of the parish', though on a less happy occasion he protested that 'I would have been glad…to have been living under a woodside to have kept a flock of sheep, rather than to have undertaken such a place as this'. Cromwell and his senior colleagues moved quickly in December 1653 to establish a new government by a written constitution, called the Instrument of Government, which had been written by a group of senior officers. It appointed Cromwell Lord Protector for life and defined his position and powers, while also guaranteeing a return to more normal, elected parliaments. Cromwell remained in office as Protector for almost five years until his death in September 1658. As both head of state and commander-in-chief of the army, Cromwell now held potentially huge power to pursue his agenda and advance his policies, though in practice he was hedged about by limitations and difficulties, and his record as Protector was mixed. However, there is no doubt that Cromwell's position changed massively in December 1653 and that thenceforth he exercised a degree of power and influence all the more remarkable when we recall that just twenty years before he had been a struggling, obscure tenant farmer in a small Cambridgeshire town.

Cromwell's appointment as Protector of England, Wales, Scotland and

Previous page: In 1653–54 the new regime struck a medal to mark its inauguration. It featured a bust of Cromwell and an inscription recording that he was Protector by the grace of God. The reverse showed the Protectoral and Cromwell family arms and a Latin motto meaning 'peace is sought through war'.
British Museum

One of the first acts of the new regime was to issue a proclamation telling the people that government was now to be by 'a Lord Protector and successive triennial parliaments' and that Cromwell had been declared Lord Protector 'and hath accepted thereof'.
The British Library, 21b.14 (40)

Ireland creates difficulties for a biographer. The flow of personal letters of the war years, already greatly diminished after Worcester, dwindled to a trickle during the Protectorate, replaced by a stream of impersonal state letters, signed by Cromwell but written by others. Far more revealing are the speeches which Cromwell delivered to his Protectorate parliaments. Moreover, with Cromwell's elevation to head of state he became just one part of the mechanism of central government and it is difficult to distinguish his own role, power, preferences and initiatives from the work of the regime as a whole. But the effort must be made, for unless we assume that in practice Protector Cromwell held unlimited power and that all political initiatives and policies stemmed directly and almost exclusively from Cromwell himself – and it will be argued that this is doubtful – a biographical study cannot become merely a political history of central government.

In some ways it is easy to keep Cromwell in sight, for throughout the Protectorate he was the conspicuous figurehead of the regime. He presided on state occasions, opening and closing parliaments, hosting or attending grand banquets, receiving ambassadors and other dignitaries. He was assigned several former royal properties, though he used only two. Whitehall Palace became his principal seat, and he, his wife, his aged mother and unmarried daughters, moved

into newly decorated apartments there in spring 1654. However, he also employed Hampton Court as a semi-rural retreat west of London, especially at weekends. Both palaces were richly redecorated with furniture and works of art, some of them royal possessions still held by the state, others acquired specifically for the Protector. He was attended by a growing and increasingly elaborate court, modelled on the traditional royal court. Unlike Stuart heads of state, Protector Cromwell was not peripatetic and he always remained in and around London, with trips to Hampton Court and the City. But he was visible in other ways. He distributed portraits and issued in his name and often over his signature charters, letters patent, proclamations and declarations; he appointed officials and ambassadors and distributed honours, including knighthoods, baronetcies and a handful of hereditary peerages; he began signing himself 'Oliver P' for Oliver Protector in imitation of the traditional royal signature; and he was referred to as 'Your Highness' or 'His Highness'. His image on horseback appeared on great seals and his bust, crowned with a laurel wreath, on coinage. As Protector, in several ways Cromwell played the role of a traditional early modern monarch and many Protectoral forms were modelled on monarchical precedents.

However, because he held office under a written constitution and was required to work within parameters set out there, on paper Cromwell possessed nothing like the powers of Stuart monarchs. The original constitution of December 1653, the Instrument of Government, and the revised version prepared by parliament in 1657, the Humble Petition and Advice, both ensured that Cromwell was a substantial head of state. Appointed for life and removable only by death, he was allocated palaces and land and granted an assured sum to run the civil and ceremonial aspects of government; he was the font of justice and had power to pardon; all magistracy and honours derived from him; and under the revised constitution he gained power to nominate his successor and appoint a new second parliamentary chamber. But in key areas of government, especially deploying the armed forces, appointing senior officers of state and raising and spending state revenues, he had no independent power and could not act alone. Instead, both constitutions stressed that the Protector could act only with the consent of parliament if sitting, or of a permanent executive council in the intervals between parliaments. The constitutions deliberately divided powers between the arms of government. Extensive though not unlimited legislative powers, together with supervisory powers over the Protector and executive, were vested in an assured succession of parliaments, initially comprising a single elected chamber, though later a second, nominated house was added; the constitutions ensured that parliaments would meet quite regularly and that each would enjoy a minimum lifespan. Extensive though not unlimited executive powers, together with supervisory powers over the Protector, were vested in a permanent executive council, which kept government running during parliamentary sessions but came into its own in the intervals between parliaments.

Cromwell seems generally to have abided by these constitutional limitations and sought consent of other bodies as required. He summoned two Protectorate

parliaments, in 1654–55 and 1656–58, and although relations with both were
sometimes rocky and in the end he angrily dissolved them, he also genuinely
tried to work with them. In particular, he followed his constitutional duty in
seeking parliament's approval of appointments to senior offices of state, the
direction of foreign policy, the making of war and the handling of state finance.
He rendered financial accounts to both and, when needing extra income, he
generally looked to parliament for help. He summoned parliament when required
to do so, observed the minimum parliamentary lifespan guaranteed by the
constitutions and, so long as MPs worked within the constitution, he ensured
they operated freely and without threat or interruption.

It is much harder to reconstruct his relations with the executive council, for
they met in private and there is much less evidence about the division of power

between them. We know that Cromwell worked closely with the council, attending part or all of around 40 per cent of the 800 or so formal meetings, as well as conferring with councillors at informal gatherings. When illness caused Cromwell to miss a run of meetings, major items were occasionally deferred until he returned; more often, the range and quantity of business continued undiminished and on his return Cromwell usually gave assent to a backlog of council decisions finalised in his absence, suggesting that Cromwell trusted the council. In several speeches Cromwell was insistent that he was working closely with his council and observing the constitutional restraints. Thus in September 1654 he stressed that the constitution had 'limited me and bound my hands to act nothing to the prejudice of the nations without consent of a Council until the Parliament met', asserting that in practice 'this government hath been exercised by a Council, with a desire to be faithful in all things', and he went on to praise the council as 'the trustees of the Commonwealth, in all intervals of parliament; who have as absolute a negative upon the supreme officer in the said intervals, as the Parliament hath whilst it is sitting. It cannot be made use of, a man cannot be raised nor a penny charged upon the people, nothing can be done without consent of Parliament; and in the intervals of Parliament, without consent of the Council it is not to be exercised'. Later in the 1650s, he referred more bitterly to the constitution as rendering him like 'a child in its swaddling clouts...I can do nothing but in ordination with the Council'. If this was all deception, it ran deep, for two key restrictions imposed on the Protector by the revised constitution of 1657 – that during the intervals of parliament he should obtain conciliar consent before appointing senior officers of state and spending state money – were not in parliament's original draft but sprang from a 'paper of objections', probably drawn up by the Protector and amended in Cromwell's own hand. His speech to a

'this government hath been exercised
by a Council, with a desire to be
faithful in all things'

parliamentary committee supporting financial oversight as 'a safety to whom-soever is your supreme Magistrate, as well as security to the public, that the monies might be issued out by the advice of the Council', is consistent with comments Cromwell made several times to different audiences, that he felt uneasy at the unlimited power which passed to him in April and December 1653, fearful of its corrupting potential, and relieved when arrangements were in place to limit his powers.

In some areas Cromwell may have deferred to the council. Power to vet newly elected MPs and exclude unqualified Members was vested in the council alone, and in theory the Protector had no part in it. In the end, councillors used their powers sparingly in summer 1654, to exclude a handful of notorious royalists or adulterers, but far more extensively and controversially in summer 1656, to exclude roughly 100 political opponents. Cromwell kept his distance, perhaps disapproving or uneasy. His attendance at council meetings dropped markedly when the election returns were considered and he was absent from those at which final decisions were probably taken. In both 1654 and 1656 a handful of excluded MPs complained to the Protector, but in response he stressed that he had neither power nor say in the business and referred them to the council. To one such, he replied that exclusion 'was an act of the Council's, and that he did not concern himself in it'. When councillor MPs defended the mass exclusions in September 1656, they repeatedly asserted that it was council business and made no reference to the Protector's involvement. Again, surviving evidence throws light on the decision in summer 1656 to call the second Protectorate parliament, taken by Protector and council only after several weeks of heated debate, in which alternative ways to meet the regime's debts were explored. Several contemporaries suggested that Cromwell and a group of councillors

Opposite: Philip Jones, portrayed here by an unknown artist, had played little part in the fighting of the 1640s, but during the 1650s he became a close colleague of Cromwell and served as a Protectoral Councillor. One of the most influential figures in central government, he also monopolised power in his native South Wales, amassed a huge fortune and acquired a mansion in the Vale of Glamorgan. *Fonman Castle, South Wales. By kind permission of Sir Brooke Boothby*

initially opposed calling parliament, and both council members as well as the less reliable Venetian ambassador – who claimed that Cromwell cried in council and decamped to Hampton Court to get away from councillors who favoured a parliament – reported long, heated debates before at length Cromwell was won over and persuaded to issue writs. Perhaps unhappy, seeking God or even sulking, Cromwell then absented himself from most council meetings over the following month. Certainly, in later outbursts he gave the impression that he had been bullied into calling parliament by his council – 'as also of his calling this Parliament, whereunto, being advised by his Council, he yielded, though he professed it, in his own judgment, no way seasonable' and 'he was against the calling of the late Parliament. But the Council urged it so'.

Although Protector Cromwell generally abided by the constitutions, sought and obtained the consent of parliament and council where required, respected their independent position and may even occasionally have been deflected from his preferred path by the council, the image he sometimes projected of himself – as puppet dancing attendance to parliament and council, hemmed in by constitutional restrictions – is implausible. Contemporary opinion that he towered over the Protectorate, dominating government, is almost certainly correct. In practice, a parliament which might be in session for just a few months every three years was in no position to challenge Cromwell. Even the council was no match for Cromwell, for he probably helped select its founder-members in December 1653 – a mixture of military and civilian colleagues, some experienced politicians and worthy provincial administrators, leavened with a couple of minor peers – and the revised constitution of summer 1657 left him free to name new councillors. Cromwell took the opportunity to drop and dismiss from all offices John Lambert, the most powerful and independent-

minded councillor and army officer of the opening years of the Protectorate. Moreover, as commander-in-chief, Cromwell had enormous potential powers and, although the military presence was not overplayed and the regime showed a civilian face, Cromwell took care to keep the army loyal to him and it, in turn, gave him an unchallengeable power-base. Many of the key domestic decisions stemmed largely or wholly from Cromwell, including the dissolutions of both Protectorate parliaments, the use of military force temporarily to close the first Protectorate parliament and the rejection of the crown but acceptance of the remainder of the 1657 constitution. Although the council and individual councillors played a part in foreign policy and diplomacy, Cromwell's was probably the dominant voice. His perception of God's will shaped his foreign and commercial as well as his domestic policies and the major foreign initiative, to make war on Spain, probably emanated from Cromwell. One of the few surviving records of a council debate shows Cromwell overcoming opposition and pushing through his view that the regime should attack Spain's colonies, and he took personal responsibility for the ensuing war and military setbacks.

During the Protectorate, as before, Cromwell was pulled in different directions. His conservative inclinations led him to make the keynote of several speeches healing and settling, and shaped policies supported or initiated by him, including the restoration of semi-monarchical forms; the return to elected parliaments and a desire for parliamentary endorsement of the Protectoral constitution; a lowering of taxes in the first half of the Protectorate, though that plunged the regime into debt; and a slow reduction in the size of the army. It is also seen in the regime's generally mild and cautious attitude, its sparing use of special courts or capital sentences against political opponents, and Cromwell's inclusive approach, seeking to win over critics and former enemies. However,

Cromwell also retained his radical inclinations, his burning desire to bring the nation and its people closer to God, thereby fulfilling God's will and repaying the Lord for His favours. As before, this entailed a broad programme of godly reformation, including securing liberty of conscience for Protestants and pursuing social, judicial and moral reform. These goals appeared repeatedly in Cromwell's speeches, where he stressed the pursuit of liberty, 'our civil liberties, as men; our spiritual liberties, as Christians'. This radical side of Cromwell kept him tied to the army, God's chosen instrument and a well of godliness, and also underpinned his rejection of the crown in 1657. Although Cromwell's confidence and enthusiasm were shaken by specific setbacks – the failure of the first Protectorate parliament in 1654–55, the royalist rebellions of spring 1655 and the defeat of the naval expedition to the Caribbean soon after – and trimmed by increasing age and declining health, Cromwell never abandoned his faith in God or his pursuit of godly reformation, and he retained a radical edge to the end.

When the Protectorate was inaugurated, Cromwell and his council were given nearly nine months to establish the regime and its policies before the first Protectorate parliament was to meet. Recognising that this period would be difficult but crucial, the constitution gave the Protector and council temporary powers until parliament met to make new laws or ordinances. Cromwell and his council worked vigorously over these months and achieved much at home and abroad. Peace was made with the Dutch, formally ending a naval war launched by the Rump, and commercial or diplomatic alliances were secured with Continental powers; throughout the Protectorate, Cromwell and his council strove to protect and promote trade and commerce. The semi-military English administrations of Scotland and Ireland were overhauled and ordinances attempted to reform Irish and Scottish civil and judicial structures and tie them more closely to, and make them more consistent with, English procedures. Over 180 ordinances were passed by Protector and council, many relating to private or local business, but some instituting important domestic reforms consistent with Cromwell's overarching goal of godly reformation. Judicial reforms included changes to the Courts of Chancery and Admiralty and to the laws dealing with creditors, debtors and poor prisoners. Protector and Council sought to regularise religious appointments, establishing procedures and bodies of commissioners – dubbed 'triers' and 'ejectors' – to vet candidates for vacant livings and review the suitability of those already in place. Cromwell was involved in initiating or finalising many ordinances, which needed his assent, and he vetoed or sent back to council for amendment a small number of draft ordinances. He strongly commended the whole reform programme to the 1654 parliament and in several later speeches he picked out for praise the system of triers and ejectors, appearing particularly proud of it and personally identifying himself with this initiative.

Cromwell opened his first Protectorate parliament in early September 1654 with an optimistic speech, referring to 'the greatest occasion that, I believe, England ever saw' and 'such a door of hope opened by God to us'. Having reviewed the achievements of the previous months, Cromwell claimed that further work by parliament would bring 'this ship of the Commonwealth...into a safe harbour' so that 'through the blessing of God you may enter into rest and peace'. But at one point Cromwell considered the bleak alternative – 'if this day, that is this meeting, prove not healing, what shall we do?' He soon had to address that question, for during the opening week republican MPs launched fierce, destructive attacks upon the new constitution and regime. In response, on 12 September Cromwell employed troops to close the House and summoned MPs to a second, sharper speech, in which he strongly defended his office and

This is one of the more important ordinances passed by Protector and Council in 1653–54, an ordinance of April 1654, based upon an old bill drafted by the Rump, to unite Scotland with England and bring various Scottish forms and practices into line with those of England. From *An Ordinance for Uniting Scotland into One Commonwealth with England*, 1654. The British Library, 21b.15 (13)

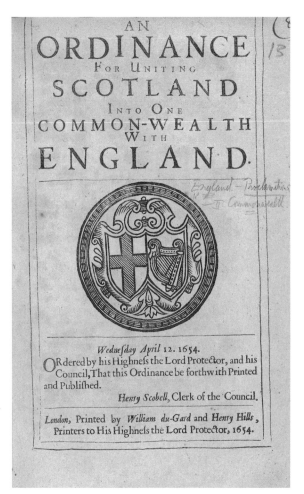

regime, told Members that though they might revise the written constitution they must respect its basic structure, and informed them that they would not be allowed back into the House until they signed a document accepting the fundamental points of the Instrument of Government. Around eighty opponents of the regime felt unable to sign and were excluded. After this stuttering start, the session did continue until January and was dominated by work on a Government Bill, designed to supersede the constitution of December 1653. This bill did incorporate many elements of the Instrument and largely adhered to the fundamentals set out by Cromwell, but in some areas it proved unsatisfactory. In particular, it seemed to narrow the liberty of conscience guaranteed by the Instrument, herald a dramatic reduction in the size of the army by slashing the military budget and permit parliament alone to gain future control of the army. Acting at the earliest possible moment permitted by the constitution, on 22 January 1655 Cromwell dissolved parliament, thereby killing its incomplete Government Bill, dismissing MPs with an angry speech highlighting their failure to make 'good and wholesome laws' and the resulting 'dissettlement and division, discontent and dissatisfaction, together with real dangers to the whole [nation and people]'. In truth, Cromwell probably shared responsibility, for he misjudged parliament's mood and was unprepared for the opposition, and attempts by him and his agents in the House, especially councillor MPs, to manage the session appear to have been limited, fitful and unsuccessful. Cromwell seems to have felt that, as Protector, he should stand aloof from parliaments and their proceedings.

In many ways the failure of the first Protectorate parliament heralded a turning point, when optimism gave way to pessimism, a programme of reform to ad hoc responses to unexpected problems. In March 1655 the regime faced its biggest direct challenge at home, a series of royalist risings, the largest in the south and south-west, though in the end all were crushed quite easily by the army. In spring and summer 1655 senior judges questioned the standing of the regime and several individuals the legality of Protectoral taxes, challenges overcome only by crude tactics – judges were sacked or pushed into resigning and individuals cowed by threatening them and their legal counsel with imprisonment. Around the same time a naval expedition sent to attack Spain in the Caribbean was heavily defeated around San Domingo in Hispaniola; though its acquisition of Jamaica instead proved in time enormously valuable, initially it was seen as very little consolation. Moreover, by late 1655 the regime was slipping deep into debt. Cromwell was deeply affected by many of these setbacks. To an old army colleague he wrote of 'wounds' and 'reproaches and anger from some of all sorts', of God's people 'being divided in opinion and too much in affection ready to fall foul upon one another'. In May 1655 he was distressed by news of a Catholic massacre of Protestants in Piedmont and when, a few weeks later, word of the Hispaniola disaster reached Cromwell, it triggered an intense and personal crisis. Cromwell saw Hispaniola as a divine rebuke, signalling that the nation, its people, the regime and perhaps Cromwell himself had displeased God and strayed into sin – 'No doubt but we have provoked the Lord and it is good for us to know so, and to be abased for the same'. Cromwell believed that, as the Lord 'hath very sorely chastened us', his people needed to 'humble ourselves before the Lord' and 'lay our mouths in the dust'. He responded by re-emphasising the urgency of measures against 'all manner of vice' and promoting 'virtue and godliness' and he re-examined his own record to ensure that he had not been corrupted by personal ambition.

OLIVARIVS PRIMVS

Yet Cromwell always felt that the Lord would restore His favour. Early in 1655 he wrote of his troubles that 'the Lord will not let it be always so', he saw the defeat of the royalist rebels as 'a blessing of God...the hand of God going along with us' and in the wake of Hispaniola he was very anxious to detect God's renewed favour, in 1657 interpreting a naval success in the Canaries as a sign of God's blessing 'according to the wonted goodness and loving-kindness of the

Lord'. Moreover, the period 1655–56 also saw new or developing policies, often shaped or promoted by Cromwell himself. Late in 1655 he initiated a conference to consider the readmission of the Jews to England, something he clearly favoured, and although strong opposition prevented their formal readmission, in practice Cromwell allowed some to settle. Liberty of conscience for Protestants was also promoted, Cromwell telling parliament in September 1656 'that which hath been our practice since the last Parliament hath been to let all this nation see that whatever pretensions be to religion, if quiet, peaceable, they may enjoy conscience and liberty to themselves, so long as they do not make religion a pretence for arms and blood'. But the most radical initiative of this period occurred in autumn 1655, when Cromwell and his council instituted a new, semi-military system of regional government in England and Wales under Major-Generals. Their instructions show that the system had several purposes – to clamp down on royalists and other opponents of the regime; to reduce sin and sinful opportunities and promote godly reformation; and to raise a new cavalry militia, funded from a new tax on wealthier royalists, which might allow modest reductions in the size and costs of the regular army. The council's work to establish the Major-Generals was held up for several weeks in late summer, when Cromwell was absent through illness, and was not completed until he returned in early autumn, perhaps a sign that Cromwell had an important role in establishing the system. He defended the Major-Generals vigorously in several speeches of 1656, praising both the security and reformist aspects of their work. Indeed, although the achievement of the Major-Generals was rather patchy, depending in part upon the varying ability, enthusiasm and workload of the individual officers, they did largely succeed in suppressing rather feeble royalist activity and thus bolstering the security of the regime; some made limited headway in reducing opportunities for sin. It may have been assurances from the Major-Generals in summer 1656 that they could ensure the orderly election of a supportive parliament which helped overcome Cromwell's initial reluctance and persuaded him to call another parliament.

In many ways the first session of the second Protectorate parliament, which ran from mid-September 1656 to late June 1657, was remarkably successful, all the more compliant because of the mass exclusion of potentially critical MPs by the council. Although there were signs of drift during the autumn, suggesting that once more Cromwell did not guide the session, in due course MPs addressed many of the concerns he had raised in his opening speech, supporting the war against Spain, voting extra money to finance that conflict and the regime and working on new legislation, some of it advancing godly reformation. Cromwell was clearly angry when in December 1656 MPs harshly punished an over-enthusiastic Quaker, James Naylor, for alleged 'horrid blasphemy', fearful that it might lead to parliamentary-backed persecution of other religious figures or minorities, but his only direct response was to question their legal authority to act thus. He appeared strangely unmoved when, in January 1657, parliament rejected a bill to authorise the new tax upon royalists to fund the new militia and the Major-Generals' system as a whole, thereby effectively ending that experiment. Although he continued to praise what the Major-Generals had achieved while in power in 1655–56, he did not strive to support them and, seemingly an indecisive bystander, he accepted parliament's decision. He was equally unmoved during the spring when parliament prepared a revised constitution to supersede the Instrument of Government. He welcomed parliamentary endorsement of the regime, by this stage he recognised that the Instrument was imperfect and in need of revision – in a furious outburst to army

This contemporary engraving shows Cromwell's reinvestiture in Westminster Hall on 26 June 1657, during which the Speaker of the House of Commons presented the Protector with an ermine-lined velvet robe, a gilt and embossed bible, a sword of state and a newly made solid gold sceptre. From *A Further Narrative of the Passages of these Times in the Commonwealth of England*, 1658.
The British Library, G3281

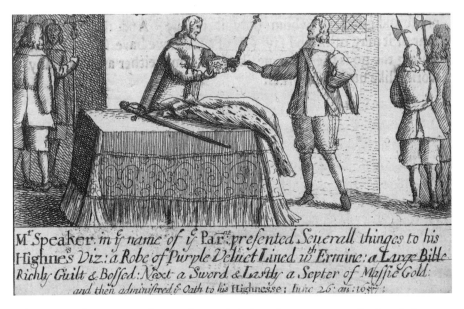

officers in February 1657 he condemned their resistance to constitutional change and, probably with the Naylor case in mind, dismissed the Instrument as 'an imperfect thing which will neither preserve our religious or civil rights' – and he welcomed most of the new constitution, which made limited changes to the existing system and which safeguarded all the fundamentals to which he had drawn attention in September 1654.

However, the parliamentary constitution contained 'one or two considerations that do stick with me. The one is that you have named me by another title than that I now bear'. Parliament's proposal to restore kingship and give Cromwell the crown led to intense heart-searching and for several weeks Cromwell agonised over what he should do, before firmly rejecting the crown

As part of the reinvestiture ceremony, Cromwell took an oath to serve as head of state. It is recorded that the oath, which was read to Cromwell by the Speaker, had been written on a piece of vellum, and it is possible that this is the original copy as used by Protector and Speaker on 26 June.
The British Library, Egerton MS 1048, f.115

The Lord Protectors Oath.

I doe in the Presence and by the name of God Almighty promise and sweare That to the vttermost of my Power I will vphold and mainteyne the true Reformed Protestant Christian Religion in the purity thereof as it is conteyned in the holy Scriptures of the old and New Testament to the vttermost of my Power and Vnderstanding and encourage the Profession, and Professors of the same. And that to the vtmost of my Power I will endeavour as Cheife Magistrate of these three Nations the maintenance and preservacon of the Peace and Safetie and of the iust rights and priviledges of the People thereof, And shall in all things according to my best Knowledge and Power governe the People of these Nations according to Law.

on 8 May. Parliament, though disappointed, agreed to continue the office of Protector, and with that amendment Cromwell accepted the Humble Petition and Advice. On 26 June he was re-installed as Protector under the new parliamentary constitution and around the same time he prorogued parliament for seven months. The decision to accept or reject the crown rested with Cromwell alone and it was clearly difficult and personal. The possible restoration of kingship aroused intense opposition in the army and Cromwell may have declined it through fear of military unrest, but he never shied away from confronting opposition and indiscipline in the army and it would have been out of character for him to have acted thus. Although tempted by kingship as another step towards restoring known and traditional forms, an aid to settlement, he may at length have rejected it through fear that it would tie him too closely to conservative forms, policies and politicians, thereby undermining and weaning

During the eighteenth century, Cromwell's descendants assembled and cherished a small collection of personal items which they believed had once been owned by Cromwell. These items are from that collection and, although strictly contemporary evidence is thin, they probably date from the mid-seventeenth century and may once have been in Cromwell's personal possession. The ornate powder flask is inlaid with ivory, amber and mother of pearl; the richly jewelled pendant carrying a bust of Cromwell may have been intended as a gift to foreign dignitaries, for the Protectoral regime employed a jeweller and in 1656 'a fair jewel with his Highness's picture' was given by Cromwell to the departing Swedish ambassador; while the ebony perfume cabinet, made in Florence, was reputedly given to Cromwell by the Duke of Tuscany in exchange for a portrait of the Protector.

The Cromwell Museum, Huntingdon

him from the still incomplete work of godly reformation. Fear that the crown might tempt him into pride and ambition may have played a part, though this comes through less clearly in his speeches. Instead, Cromwell's speeches suggest that rejection was grounded on his interpretation of God's will. Opposition from the army, God's chosen instrument, and from good and godly individuals, swayed Cromwell – 'I cannot think that God would bless me in the undertaking of anything, that would justly and with cause grieve them'. Moreover, he believed that in winter 1648–49 God had spoken against the office of king as well as the person of Charles I – 'Truly the providence of God has laid this title aside providentially…God has seemed providentially not only to strike at the family but at the name'. Cromwell concluded that he must adhere to the Lord's destruction of monarchy – 'I would not seek to set up that that providence hath destroyed and laid in the dust, and I would not build Jericho again'.

The last year of Cromwell's life is often portrayed as a period of drift and failure, as old age, ill health and disappointment took their toll. Certainly, there were few new policy initiatives and several failures. Thus the second session of the second Protectorate parliament was brief – from 20 January to 4 February 1658 – and entirely unproductive, for the Commons, dominated by Members excluded in September 1656 but now admitted, tore into the regime and the new nominated second chamber which Cromwell had appointed the previous autumn. Cromwell dissolved parliament with a speech which was not just bitter and angry but also briefer than his earlier orations, probably a reflection of declining health. With no new parliamentary taxes agreed, during 1658 the regime again sank deeper into debt and financial crisis loomed. But in contrast, this period also saw a string of military successes against Spain, both in the Caribbean, where Britain's seizure of Jamaica was confirmed, and in alliance with France on the near Continent, with Britain taking control of Dunkirk; the foreign and commercial policies were continuing to bear fruit. Cromwell retained tight control over the army to the end, with another purge of malcontents early in 1658. When he opened his last parliamentary session his speech, though brief, contained signs of optimism about the future, noting that despite all the disappointments 'sometimes God pardoneth nations also. And if the enjoyment of our present peace and other mercies may be witnesses for God, we feel and we see them every day'. Although we possess only brief summaries, Cromwell was still able to deliver robust and cogent speeches to the army and to the City dignitaries during the spring and summer, before his health gave way. Cromwell had suffered intermittent bouts of illness for years, but several commentators noticed a more serious physical decline in 1657–58. Upset by the death of his favourite daughter in early August 1658, Cromwell's health collapsed soon after and a series of sharp, malaria-type fevers led to his own death during the afternoon of 3 September, his lucky day, the anniversary of Dunbar and Worcester, a few months short of his sixtieth birthday.

Cromwell's record as Protector was mixed. Like many politicians, he found the high ideals and purity of opposition sometimes giving way to messy

'I would not seek to set up that that providence hath destroyed and laid in the dust, and I would not build Jericho again'

compromises and entanglements in power. He must bear some responsibility for the use of imprisonment or exile without trial, the imposition of the Major-Generals and the new, unparliamentary tax upon royalists, the closing of parliament and the novel test set MPs on 12 September 1654, if not the mass exclusion of Members in September 1656, as well as the reimposition of state censorship effected in autumn 1655. His speeches to parliament sometimes stretched truth and twisted facts to cast himself in a good light and lay blame elsewhere, and his repeated assertions that he was an unwilling head of state – 'I called not myself to this place', 'I begged to be dismissed of my charge, I begged it again and again', 'know, I sought not this place, I speak it before God, angels and men, I did not' and so on – must have jarred with many contemporaries. For all his attempts to reassure and reconcile, Cromwell's Protectorate was ultimately quite a narrowly based regime kept in power by the army, disliked by royalists, Presbyterians, politicians alienated by the treatment of the Long Parliament and its Rump in December 1648 and April 1653 and republicans and some religious radicals who saw the Protectorate as a betrayal of the good old cause. Yet it did provide a period of mild, stable, orderly government, restoring many traditional forms, attempting to reconcile and reunite, thus laying foundations for healing and settling, and it ensured that the nation was peaceful at home and strong abroad. Cromwell's humility, springing from his faith and perhaps his modest background, together with his desire for godly reformation, for the people to enter a new Promised Land, ensured that he remained a radical, sought progress and improvement, and, unlike many post-revolutionary leaders, never became a self-interested, power-mad, bloodthirsty tyrant. Cromwell's reputation as Protector ultimately rests not so much on the mixed achievements of his government but on the inherent decency of the man and his regime.

Conclusion

'Lord, though I am a miserable and wretched creature, I am in Covenant with Thee through grace. And I may, I will, come to Thee, for Thy People. Thou hast made me, though very unworthy, a mean instrument to do them some good, and Thee service'
(from what is reputed to be Cromwell's last prayer, September 1658)

Soon after reputedly uttering this final prayer, Cromwell died at Whitehall Palace. His imperfectly embalmed body was quietly buried in a vault in Westminster Abbey, leaving the great ceremonies of the autumn – the lying and standing in state and the state funeral of 23 November – to one or more moveable effigies of wood and wax and an empty coffin. After the Restoration, a vengeful royalist parliament had many of those who had signed Charles I's death warrant in January 1649 hunted down, tried and executed, but they also decided that the bodies of a few of the leading regicides who had already died should be disinterred and butchered. Thus in January 1661, on the twelfth anniversary of Charles I's execution, Cromwell's was one of a handful of corpses exhumed and posthumously hanged and decapitated at Tyburn. His trunk was dumped in a pit at Tyburn, now the Marble Arch area, while his severed head was for a time displayed but then became a gruesome collector's item, examined, sketched and photographed, until in 1960 the semi-mummified skull believed to be Cromwell's was bequeathed to Sidney Sussex, his old Cambridge college, and immured in the chapel.

The barbarity of January 1661 reflects one side of contemporary opinion, the negative views which occasionally found their way into print during Cromwell's lifetime but which poured from the presses following his death and the Restoration and which continued to dominate published assessments through to the nineteenth century. Thus for one contemporary author Cromwell was 'the

Previous page: There are many versions of this three-quarter-length portrait of Cromwell by Robert Walker and his school, dating from the very late 1640s or early 1650s. This version was probably originally painted for and owned by Cromwell's daughter Bridget, who had married Henry Ireton in 1646. *The Cromwell Museum, Huntingdon*

Opposite: Although Cromwell's body was buried soon after his death, during autumn 1658 mourners were able to view a full-size effigy of the late Protector, lying in state in Somerset House. The effigy was very regally dressed, and a crown sat on a chair of state by the bed. From *Some Farther Intelligence of the Affairs of England*, 1659. *The British Library, C.55.c.9*

Devil of later times, who Butcher-like made cruelty his profession and was never better than when he had his sword sheathed in his Countrymen's bowels', while another alleged that, when reminded of the people's rights enshrined in Magna Carta, Cromwell contemptuously dismissed it as 'Magna Farta'. A pamphlet of 1665 colourfully described Cromwell as 'this wicked monster,...the centre of mischief, a shame to the British chronicle, a blot to gentility, a pattern for tyranny, whose horrid treasons will scarce gain credit with posterity, whose bloody tyranny will quite drown the names of Nero, Domitian, Caligula, etc'. However, the more positive views of Cromwell, which have increasingly dominated serious historical and biographical works from the nineteenth century onwards, find their origins in some contemporary assessments. For example, in a laudatory biography published just a few months after Cromwell's death, Richard Flecknoe portrayed him as a surgeon who had healed the wounds of civil war, a visionary who had advanced civil and religious liberties, and a great man who, 'Atlas-like', not only supported the nation but had also made function the disjointed elements of the post-civil war state. Dismissing contemporary criticisms of Cromwell as mere 'envy and malice', Flecknoe concluded 'that a Greater and more Excellent personage had no where been produc't by this latter Age; nor (perhaps) in our Nation by any former ones'.

Although no contemporary funerary monument to Cromwell survives, we can approach him in other ways. We lack contemporary likenesses of the early Cromwell, for down to the 1640s he was insufficiently wealthy or important to commission or merit a portrait, but from around 1646 until his death he featured in a range of likenesses, subtle or crude, admiring or satirical, engraved, painted or cast. In particular we have portraits or miniatures by three of the greatest artists then working in England, Robert Walker, Sir Peter Lely and Samuel Cooper,

showing Cromwell in his closing decade, with long but thinning hair, thickening jowls and waist, a slight moustache and a tuft of hair below his lip, wearing fairly simple clothes or armour and no jewellery. We also have several descriptions of Cromwell by those who met or worked with him. Sir Philip Warwick later recalled Cromwell's simple, almost crude appearance, as an MP in the early 1640s, 'very ordinarily apparelled,…[in] a plain cloth-suit, which seemed to have been made by an ill country tailor', his linen 'plain, and not very clean', with specks of blood on his collar, 'his countenance swollen and reddish, his voice sharp and untuneable'. Much later, in 1655, the Venetian ambassador noted the 'very scanty beard, of sanguine complexion, medium stature, robust, of martial presence'. But the fullest description came from a servant, John Maidstone, who also noted his 'compact and strong' physique, 'his stature under 6 foote (I beleeve about two inches)', but who focused on Cromwell's mental and emotional state, recalling the 'exceeding fyery' temper, though 'the flame of it kept downe, for the most part, or soon allayed', a man of great courage but also 'naturally compassionate', of great 'tendernesse towards sufferers'. 'A larger soul, I thinke, hath seldome dwelt in a house of clay than his was'.

Sr I was not what hopd to haue
bene with you this night, but truelye
my aged mother is in such a condition
of illnesse, that I could not leaue her
with satisfaction. I expected to haue had
the Deedes sealed herein with were to bee
performed on my part, but my Lawyer
tells mee that it wilbe most necessarie for
mee to bee with you att the doeing
thereof, I haue sent them to you
by this bearer for your perusall, and I must to bee
with you vpon munday night (if God
will) I shalbe able to stay only tuse
day with you, for indeed I must ne-
cessarilyd bee back on wedensday
night, my occasionss causd thinsed
affaires to god in such a hurryd
vnbefittings the wayte of them, And
I doubt wilbe troublesome to you, w
I desire you to excuse mee in. I beseech the Lord to blesse proceedings
and to vouchsafe his presence. my
wife presents her affectionate respects

to youre selfe and Ladye, so doe I mine, And to
youre whole family
I take leaue and rest sr

youre affectionate freind and servant
W Marsh
Aprl 28
1640.

Cromwell was an emotional man, driven by a burning faith, given to periods of doubt, introspection or seeking God, contrasting with elation and exuberance at times of triumph, notably after military victories, or moments of fiery temper and sudden angry outbursts. But he tackled his workload in a sensible, rational manner and occasional attempts to portray him as a manic depressive or mentally disturbed appear unfounded. Physically, he was quite robust and healthy well into middle age, travelling great distances and campaigning vigorously in the 1640s. He emerged from the fighting almost unscathed, sustaining nothing more than a slight neck wound, at Marston Moor in July 1644. Far more troublesome were the boils, abscesses and 'impostumes' to which he was prone. By the 1650s he was suffering other afflictions, principally a recurrent fever which may have been picked up when campaigning in southern Ireland in autumn 1649 and which, compounded by dysentery, laid him low in Edinburgh for several months in 1651. Writing to his wife in autumn 1650 he admitted that 'I grow an old man, and feel infirmities of age marvellously stealing upon me' and in autumn 1655, when he was recovering from another bout of fever, the Venetian ambassador noticed that he was 'pulled in appearance' and that 'as he stood uncovered the hand holding his hat trembled'. The fevers, sweats and 'agues', the hot and cold 'fits', which wracked him for much of August 1658 and eventually killed him in September, were probably further manifestations of the malaria-like disease first contracted almost a decade before.

Cromwell enjoyed a warm family life. Although his father died when he was still in his teens, he remained very close to his mother, and she lived with him and his wife for the remainder of her long life. In 1649, as he was preparing for Ireland, Cromwell wrote that he was loath to leave her 'in such a condition of illness', though in fact she survived another five years, dying at Whitehall in autumn 1654, in her ninetieth year. He remained in contact with several of his sisters, three of whose husbands became parliamentarian officers and one of them, John Disbrowe, a close colleague. In 1651 Cromwell wrote to his unmarried sister Elizabeth, apologising for writing infrequently, sending her £20 'as a small token of my love' and signing himself 'your affectionate brother'. Cromwell's marriage was long and happy and he and his wife, who lived until 1665, had nine children between 1621 and 1639. The few surviving letters between the couple, dating from the early 1650s, reveal a deep and enduring affection. Writing from Scotland, Cromwell told his wife that 'Thou art dearer to me than any creature; let that suffice', and in another letter he assured her 'My Dearest, I could not satisfy myself to omit this post, although I have not much to write; yet indeed I love to write to my dear, who is very much in my heart', closing 'Still pray for Thine, O Cromwell'. In her one surviving letter to him, of December 1650, Elizabeth expressed a desire to see her husband again, if the Lord willed it, for 'Truly my lif is but half a lif in your abseinse'. As Lady Protectress, she played minor, supporting roles on some public occasions, but she stayed in the

On 3 May 1651 Cromwell wrote to his wife, 'My Dearest', from Edinburgh, expressing his joy in writing to and hearing of her, asking her to convey his duty to his elderly mother and sending 'my love to all the family'. He closed, 'Still pray for Thine, O Cromwell'. *The British Library, Harleian MS 6988, f.233*

background and seems to have neither held nor sought real power or a political role. Cromwell's letters also reveal a fatherly concern for his children, exhorting them to seek the Lord and avoid sin. Thus Henry was urged 'to be innocent,…roll yourself upon God…[and] take heed of being over-jealous' and newly married Bridget to 'press on; let not husband, let not anything cool thy affection after Christ'. Cromwell was particularly concerned about his eldest son Richard, whose lack of obvious godliness and fondness for good and expensive living, running up debts, he labelled 'idleness'.

The least controversial area of Cromwell's post-1640 career is his role as a soldier, for even critics have conceded that Cromwell was an outstanding military figure. Although he had no experience before 1642, he learned quickly, worked well alone or with others, paid unusual attention to the administration and financing of the war, ensured the welfare and discipline of his troops, and possessed the confidence and dynamism to seek victory in what he saw as a just and godly conflict. He was brilliant on the battlefield, seeing his enemies' weaknesses, seizing the initiative and maintaining tight control over his troops, on two occasions – around Preston and at Dunbar – defeating armies significantly outnumbering his own. He was not so adept at manoeuvre warfare, often thwarted by the Scots, and his record in sieges was more mixed, with terrible successes at Basing, Drogheda and Wexford balanced by setbacks elsewhere, especially in Ireland, with rebuffs at Duncannon and Waterford and expensive pyrrhic victories at Kilkenny and Clonmel, his blackest day. As an active officer his military career was short, spanning barely nine years from inexperienced captain in August 1642 to all-conquering Lord General in September 1651. Probably only at Dunbar and Worcester did he have overall command in battle of armies over 10,000-strong and only in summer 1650 did he become parliamentary commander-in-chief. Nonetheless, he was the most consistently successful and conspicuously dynamic general on either side during the civil wars, a natural military genius, and his achievements, though limited to Britain and Ireland, often lead to comparisons with Marlborough, Wellington or Montgomery.

Cromwell the man of God is harder to grasp, for many of his beliefs seem far removed from our day and in some areas our knowledge is very incomplete. After his conversion, Cromwell believed that he had been chosen by God for a special duty and that thereafter God guided and generally favoured him. That did not make him a puritan kill-joy of popular image – he valued recreation, smoked a pipe, took ale, enjoyed occasional lavish banquets and appreciated singing, dancing, music and art. But it did lead him both to avoid personal sin and to encourage the extirpation of sin as part of a wider programme. During the 1640s and 1650s Cromwell came to believe that the biblical story of the Israelites was being replayed, with God freeing his chosen people, the English, from the Egyptian bondage of Stuart tyranny, leading them through the blood red sea of civil war and into the wilderness of post-war uncertainty; perhaps his role was to show the people that they were impure, convince them to reform and so propel them from the wilderness towards the Garden of Eden, winning God's love and making England a second Canaan. Thus godly reformation, the purging of sins and the creation of a more godly nation, was also a means to an end. In the early 1650s Cromwell may have believed that Christ's second coming was imminent, though this millenarianism – a belief that Christ was about to return and rule on earth for a thousand years – seems to have cooled thereafter. Cromwell also had an intense belief in divine providences, with God actively intervening in the world to shape events. This led him to interpret successes as gifts from God and signs of His favour to His worthless servant, Oliver Cromwell, but failures as rebukes from the Lord and warnings that he had strayed or sinned.

While belief in millenarianism and God's providences was common amongst the godly, Cromwell's advocacy of liberty of conscience was more unusual and distinctive. His belief that each of the new Protestant groups of the period contained an element of God's truth led him to cherish Protestant plurality in the war and post-war years and passionately to advocate liberty for each group to worship and thrive, though he hoped that in time they might all naturally coalesce to reveal a complete mosaic of God's message. Disliking distinctive names, labels or denominations, he prayed for cooperation, congruity and mutual acceptance, 'to see union and right understanding between the godly people (Scots, English, Jews, Gentiles, Presbyterians, Independents, Anabaptists, and all)'. However, Cromwell's liberty did not extend to all. In theory Catholics and rigid episcopalians were excluded – though in practice those who were loyal to the regime and discreet in their worship were not harassed during the Protectorate – as were those whose faith strayed into blasphemy and heresy, who challenged the civil authorities or who benefited from such liberty only to attack other sects. Cromwell repeatedly bewailed the failure of sects to work peacefully together, bitterly condemning those who 'put their fingers upon their brethren's consciences, to pinch them there', who make 'wounds in a man's side and would desire nothing more than to be groping and grovelling with his fingers in those wounds. They will be making wounds, and rending and tearing, and making them wider than they are'.

In part, Cromwell the politician and statesman was moulded by his background and his secular ideas. Never a social revolutionary, he supported and praised the existing order – he referred to property as one of 'the badges of the kingdom of Christ' and told parliament 'A nobleman, a gentleman, a yeoman? That is a good interest of the nation and a great one' – and he strongly opposed any group apparently agitating for social overturning or military insubordination. In some ways this conservatism was reinforced by his limited intellectual outlook, for he was not a profound or original thinker – one of his earliest biographers commented that 'It is obvious to all, he studied Men more than Books' – and down to the 1640s he had limited experience of administration and politics. During the last decade or more of his life, he was sometimes guided by, or reacted to, the initiatives of others with wider experience and sharper ideas. But far more important, Cromwell's approach to politics and statesmanship was shaped by his faith and his interpretation of God's will. In his words and actions of the 1640s and 1650s Cromwell stressed that what mattered were the ends not the means and forms of government. A regime must be seen to have God's support and be working towards God's goals, chiefly godly reformation and liberty of conscience. Once Cromwell came to believe that a regime did not have God's support or was not advancing God's cause, he not only withdrew his support but also was willing to use his power to remodel or remove it. He proclaimed that he was not 'wedded and glued to forms of Government' and that all mortal governments were but 'dross and dung in comparison of Christ'.

Thus Cromwell was willing to experiment with or change secular governments in order to advance God's work. He negotiated with the king in 1647 and sought a monarchical settlement, only to support regicide and the abolition of monarchy in 1648–49, in the process acquiescing in the drastic remodelling of the Long Parliament. He then supported the Rump, only to turn against it and destroy it in spring 1653. He experimented with a Nominated Assembly, only to accept its resignation in December 1653 and subsequently condemn it as a failure. Thereafter he became head of state and presided over the Protectoral regime in the hope this would advance God's cause. Consequently, Cromwell appears profoundly inconsistent, at times stressing the sovereignty of the people and their elected parliaments, at others snarling that the important thing was the people's 'good, not what pleases them', at times stressing the sanctity of the law, at others commenting that 'if nothing should be done but what is according to law, the throat of the nation may be cut, till we send for some to make a law', at times urging caution, telling his army colleagues they must 'consider the way' as well as the end, at others intervening impulsively and with little forward planning. His political path also led him to disappoint, break with or make enemies of successive waves of allies or potential allies – Presbyterians and conservative parliamentarians by his treatment of parliament, king and monarchy in winter 1648–49, Levellers and other radical groups by his increasing opposition to their agenda in the late 1640s and early 1650s, fervent millenarian groups and their allies by dropping them and supporting more secular forms of government in the 1650s, and republicans by his ejection of the Rump, the establishment of the Protectorate and the restoration of a single head of state during 1653. But from the early 1640s, when his faith began shaping his political objectives, until his death in 1658, Cromwell consistently made the pursuit of liberty his main goal, repeatedly and emphatically pledging himself to secure 'liberty of conscience and liberty of subjects, two as glorious things to be contended for as any God hath given us'. Of the two, civil liberty was important as 'the next best thing God hath given men in the world', but for Cromwell the pursuit of religious liberty was paramount. It was the driving force behind the entire civil war – 'All the money of this nation would not have tempted men to fight, upon such an account as they have engaged, if they had not had hopes of liberty' – and the fundamental element of any godly post-war settlement – 'that of religion and the preservation of the professors thereof, to give them all due and just liberty, and to assert the truths of God'.

Cromwell's legacy is elusive, not least because it is difficult to distinguish his personal contribution from that of the parliamentary cause as a whole. In the short term, he probably nominated his elder son to succeed him and in September 1658 Richard became Lord Protector. But Cromwell had done little to prepare Richard for office and bequeathed him acute financial problems and military tensions which soon overwhelmed him. The collapse of Richard's Protectorate in spring 1659 led to a period of constitutional instability ending with the Restoration of the Stuarts and traditional monarchical government in spring 1660, whereupon Charles II reversed many of the policies of the preceding years. Taking a longer-term perspective, historians often talk about seeds sown by Cromwell, particularly as Lord Protector, which then lay dormant for several decades, before re-emerging decades later, in the late seventeenth or eighteenth centuries. The more secure position in government eventually achieved by parliament, the shift in power from crown to more established legislative and executive arms, the renewed union of Scotland and Ireland with England, and the rebuilding of England's and Britain's armed forces and the resumption of active, expansive, military-backed foreign and commercial policies all to some degree chimed with policies favoured or pursued by Cromwell in the mid-seventeenth century. On the other hand, later religious toleration was not akin to Cromwell's liberty of conscience, for Cromwell sought a liberty which would eventually lead to a reuniting of faiths, not permanent plurality and deep divisions. Moreover, a governmental programme of godly reformation in the Cromwellian sense died with him and was never resurrected. But Cromwell's real importance is not found in rather uncertain and tenuous long-term legacies. It rests in his fundamental integrity, honesty and moderation, in his unfailing desire to support, improve and work for the people and their liberties, in a trust in God and a conviction that he could achieve something positive which did not falter, even in the face of obstacles, opposition and setbacks. As he told parliament in January 1655, in the midst of disappointments but in phrases ringing with optimism and a profound faith, 'I bless God I have been inured to difficulties, and I never found God failing when I trusted in Him; I can laugh and sing in my heart when I speak of these things'.

Chronology

Spends the next twelve months campaigning with the New Model Army, including:

14 June: Battle of Naseby

10 July: Battle of Langport

July: Siege and capture of Bridgwater

August: Siege and capture of Sherborne castle

August–September: Siege and capture of Bristol

September–October: Siege and capture of Devizes and Winchester

8–14 October: Siege, storm and capture of Basing House

1646 9 January: Fight at Bovey Tracey

16 February: Battle of Torrington

March–April: Siege and capture of Exeter

May–June: Siege of Oxford

Summer: with parliamentary victory in the civil war, returns to London and to parliamentary business; moves his family to London

1647 May: Part of a delegation to the New Model Army at Saffron Walden

3 June: Leaves London to join the New Model Army around Newmarket

July: With the army at Reading and plays a prominent role in the military debates there

August: With the New Model Army as it enters London to restore order in parliament

28 October–11 November: Plays a prominent role in the military debates at Putney

15 November: Helps to crush a minor mutiny at Corkbush Field in Hertfordshire

1648 30 April: Commands part of the New Model Army sent to crush rebellion in South Wales

24 May–11 July: Siege and capture of Pembroke

July–August: Moves north to engage the Scottish-royalist army invading England

17 August: Battle of Preston, then mops up Scottish-royalist forces in south Lancashire

September–October: Visits Scotland

November: Siege of Pontefract castle

6 December: Returns to London a few hours after Pride's Purge

1649 January: Actively supports the trial (20–27) and execution (30) of Charles I

14–15 May: Helps to crush a mutiny at Burford

1649–50 Campaigns in Ireland, including:

11 September: Storm of Drogheda

11 October: Storm of Wexford

October: Capture of New Ross

October–December: Unsuccessful sieges of Duncannon and Waterford

February: Capture of Fethard, Cashel and Cahir

March: Siege and capture of Kilkenny

16 May: Attempted storm of Clonmel repulsed, though the town then surrenders

28 June: Appointed Lord General and commander-in-chief of parliament's forces

1650–51 Campaigns in Scotland, including:

July–August: Approaches Edinburgh/Leith but draws back

3 September: Battle of Dunbar

Autumn: Approaches Stirling but draws back

Winter–spring: Based in Edinburgh; ill for much of the time

20 July: Battle of Inverkeithing

August: The Scottish-royalist army moves south and enters England

3 September: Battle of Worcester

Autumn: Active military career ends and returns to London and to parliament; he and his family assigned lodgings off Whitehall

1653 20 April: Expels the Rump parliament

29 April: A new interim Council of State established

4 July: Opens the Nominated Assembly

12 December: Accepts the resignation of the Nominated Assembly

16 December: Inaugurated as Lord Protector of Britain and Ireland

1654 Passes extensive programme of reforming ordinances

April: Peace treaty with the Dutch, one of a series of diplomatic and commercial treaties

Spring: He and his family take up residence at Whitehall Palace and Hampton Court

September: Opens (3–4), then briefly closes and purges (12) the first
Protectorate Parliament

1655 22 January: Dissolves the first Protectorate Parliament
March: Royalist risings in several parts of England
April–May: Naval expedition to Hispaniola repulsed, though Jamaica captured
Late summer/early autumn: establishes the system of the Major-Generals
Autumn: Formal declaration of war against Spain; alliance with France follows
December: Conference considers the formal readmittance of the Jews

1656 June: Decides to call another parliament
17 September: Opens the second Protectorate Parliament
December: Parliament debates Naylor's case

1657 January: Parliament debates and rejects a bill to support the Major-Generals
February–March: Parliament debates and finalises a new written constitution
8 May: After weeks of uncertainty, refuses the crown and firmly rejects the new
constitution
26 June: Accepts the new constitution once revised by parliament to retain the
office of Lord Protector; reinstalled as Protector; prorogues parliament for
seven months
October: Anglo-French victories over Spain; Spanish attempts to recover Jamaica
repulsed
Autumn: Selects founder-members of the new second parliamentary chamber

1658 20 January: Opens the second session of the second Protectorate Parliament
4 February: Dissolves the second Protectorate Parliament
June: Following further Anglo-French victories over the Spanish, English forces
occupy Dunkirk; another Spanish attempt to recover Jamaica is repulsed
August: Daughter Elizabeth dies after a long illness; own health collapses
3 September: Dies at Whitehall; succeeded as Protector by eldest son Richard
23 November: State funeral in London, ending at Westminster Abbey

1659 Spring: A military coup leads to the fall of Richard and the end of the
Protectorate

1660 Spring: The restoration of monarchy and of Charles II

1661 January: Body exhumed and posthumously hanged and decapitated at Tyburn

Further reading

The best modern biographies of Cromwell include: Christopher Hill, *God's Englishman* (Penguin, Harmondsworth, 1970); Barry Coward, *Oliver Cromwell* (Longman, Harlow, 1991); Peter Gaunt, *Oliver Cromwell* (Blackwell, Oxford, 1996); and Colin Davis, *Oliver Cromwell* (Arnold, London, 2001).

Several collections also focus on Cromwell, including: Ivan Roots, *Cromwell, A Profile* (Macmillan, London, 1973); John Morrill, *Oliver Cromwell and the English Revolution* (Longman, Harlow, 1990); and David Smith, *Cromwell and the Interregnum* (Blackwell, Oxford, 2003).

Cromwell's military career can be traced through: Clyve Holmes, *The Eastern Association in the English Civil War* (Cambridge University Press, Cambridge, 1974); and Ian Gentles, *The New Model Army in England, Ireland and Scotland, 1645-53* (Blackwell, Oxford, 1992).

Cromwell's unfolding political career 1647–53 can be followed through: Austin Woolrych, *Soldiers and Statesmen* (Clarendon, Oxford, 1987); David Underdown, *Pride's Purge* (Oxford University Press, Oxford, 1971); Blair Worden, *The Rump Parliament* (Cambridge University Press, Cambridge, 1974); and Austin Woolrych, *Commonwealth to Protectorate* (Clarendon, Oxford, 1982).

The best introduction to Cromwell and the Protectorate is Barry Coward, *The Cromwellian Protectorate* (Manchester University Press, Manchester, 2002).

Cromwell's historical reputation is discussed in several works listed above, but see also: Roger Richardson, *Images of Oliver Cromwell* (Manchester University Press, Manchester, 1993); and Blair Worden, *Roundhead Reputations* (Penguin, Harmondsworth, 2001) chapters 8–11.

Cromwell can also be approached through his own words. W.C. Abbott gathered all the then known letters and speeches in *The Writings and Speeches of Oliver Cromwell* (Harvard University Press, Cambridge, MA, 1937–47), reissued by Oxford University Press in 1988. However, a more attractive collection is Thomas Carlyle's *The Letters and Speeches of Oliver Cromwell*, first published in 1845 (Chapman & Hall, London), and frequently reissued with additional material, edited by Carlyle and later by others, which remained in print well into the twentieth century. Ivan Roots, *Speeches of Oliver Cromwell* (Dent & Sons, London, 1989) is a modern edition of the speeches, while transcripts of the army's 1647 Reading and Putney debates, in which Cromwell played a prominent role, can be found in Charles Firth, *The Clarke Papers* volumes I and II, reissued as a single volume (Royal Historical Society, London, 1992).

Index